Aubrey H. Whitehouse Series no. 3

TOPICAL CONCORDANCE

TO THE QUR'AN

TRANSLATED BY
A. WHITEHOUSE
FROM MUHAMMAD AL A RABY ALAZUZY
BEIRUT
CE 1956 - AH. 1375

Arthur Jeffery Centre for the Study of Islam
Melbourne School of Theology

An affiliated college of the Australian College of Theology

mst press
Melbourne School of Theology

Topical Concordance to the Qur'an
Translated (in part) by A.H. Whitehouse
A Concordance for the Study of Quranic Science
Muhammad al Araby al Azuzy, Beirut
CE1956 – AH 1375

ISBN 978-0-9876154-6-6

Editor
Ruth Nicholls

Production and Cover Design
Ho-yuin Chan

Publishing Services
Published by MST Press
Thank you to Richard Shumack for his publishing services.

Arthur Jeffery Centre for the Study of Islam
Melbourne School of Theology
5 Burwood Highway, Wantirna, Victoria, 3152,
Australia.
PO Box 6257, Vermont Sth., Victoria, 3152, Australia
Ph: +61 3 9881 7800, Fax: +61 3 9800 0121
info@JefferyCentre.mst.edu.au

Aubrey. H. Whitehouse Series

The volumes in the Aubrey. H. Whitehouse Series of books from MST Press and the Arthur Jeffery Centre for the Study of Islam are:

Do You Remember ...? Recollections and Reflections [1]
Aubrey H. Whitehouse

Perspectives on the Qur'an: A Collection of Essays in honour of Aubrey H. Whitehouse
Aubrey H. Whitehouse Series no. 2
Editor: Ruth J. Nicholls

Topical Concordance to the Qur'an
Aubrey H. Whitehouse Series no. 3
Trans: Aubrey H. Whitehouse (reprint)
Foreword: Ruth J. Nicholls

---

[1] This is a reflection on the author's experiences in Egypt, from 1935-1956.

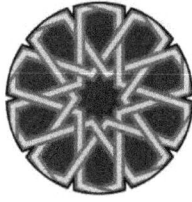

ARTHUR JEFFERY CENTRE FOR THE STUDY OF ISLAM,
Melbourne School of Theology, Australia

Formerly known as the Centre for the Study of Islam and Other Faiths it was renamed the Arthur Jeffery Centre for the Study of Islam in 2016. Arthur Jeffery was an Australian Methodist missionary who first went to India and ultimately developed proficiency in 19 languages. A contemporary of Samuel Zwemer, Jeffery became a recognized scholar of Islam who was invited to join the staff of the American University in Cairo. His book, "The Foreign Vocabulary of the Qur'an" which was first printed in 1938, still stands as the standard text in the field.

The Arthur Jeffery Centre for the Study of Islam is the only such Centre in Australia. Through its team of expert scholars and teachers of Islam it provides a variety of resources at both academic and public levels for those involved in or desiring to be involved in loving and meaningful engagement with Muslims.

The Centre is responsible for designing, preparing and teaching subjects approved by the Australian College of Theology at undergraduate and postgraduate levels relating to Islam. The Centre also aims for academic excellence through its publications which include not only scholarly works but also information for those who desire to increase their understanding of Islam. As part of its public engagement the Centre also holds open seminars and events, often joining with others sharing a similar vision and ethos. Staff are also available to speak at public programs.

In 2018 the Centre celebrates 10 years of operation and has established itself as a major centre for postgraduate studies in Islam.

For further information about the Centre and its activities, as well as opportunities to study Islam in a Christian context at both undergraduate and postgraduate levels, email info@JefferyCentre.mst.edu.au

CONTENTS

ALPHABETICAL LIST

OF CONTENTS BY SECTION

Fasting

Food, Drink, Hunting etc.

H

Historical Narratives

(Holy) Fear and Dread

Hypocrites, Unbelievers and Polytheists

J

Jihad (Holy War)

Justice, Witness (Testimony) etc.

L

Learning (Knowledge) and Science

(Legal) Almsgiving (Zakat)

Living Expenses

M

Marriage

Medicine and Anatomy

Merits of Speech

Muhammad (on him be prayers and peace)

O

Oaths and Covenants

P

People of the Book

Pilgrimage

Prayer

Purity

S

Sedition, Discord and The Last Day (The Hour)

Stories of the Prophets

T

Taking Refuge (in God)

The (Day of) Resurrection

The Unity (of God)

V

Verities and Virtues

Visions and Their Interpretations

FOREWORD

With almost 100 years of history, the Melbourne School of Theology (previously the Bible College of Victoria and prior to that the Melbourne Bible Institute) through its many students has had a significant impact in a wide variety of fields. However, that impact is more concentrated in a breadth of areas relating to the church and various forms of Christian ministry. That ministry involves responding to the Divine command of telling others about Jesus Christ: who He is, what He has done and inviting allegiance to Him. This means that this ministry has involved people crossing cultural barriers and interacting with people around the world.

While Christian missionaries have come under heavy attack for attempting to convert, change or influence people of other cultures and impose (so it is said) on them Western values and culture, many, many missionaries have been at the forefront of preserving cultures, particularly in their spoken form, often being the first to reduce a language to writing where there has been no written script. Producing dictionaries and grammars as well as developing literacy has played a significant part in attempts to relate meaningfully and culturally to people. The goal has been to interact with that particular people group in their own language and encourage literacy in their very own language. This is a very different approach from Islam which demands that its adherents read, write and speak Arabic to the (almost) exclusion of their own original languages (cf. Egypt, Syria, Iraq).

In their desire to relate deeply and meaningfully to the culture and the religion with which they are interacting, many missionaries have done extensive studies of the culture and its language, often becoming experts in the field. Many of those who have gone to Muslim countries have become recognized scholars of Islam: Samuel Zwemer, Temple Gairdner, Arthur Jeffery, Montgomery Watt, Kenneth Cragg, Kenneth Bailey to name just a few. One of the graduates of the Melbourne School of Theology (then the Melbourne Bible Institute) Aubrey Whitehouse went to Egypt as a

1

Christian missionary. There he committed himself to the study of Arabic and Islam. His achievements include writing a *Basic Arabic Course* which had accompanying cassettes, as well as a teach-yourself *Introduction to Islam.* In order to help those who wanted to meaningfully study the Qur'an, Whitehouse translated an Arabic Concordance of the Qur'an primarily to assist those studying the Qur'an to understand how Muslims themselves consider and categorise its contents. His efforts were published in a small pocket-sized booklet, a copy of which I personally owned.

When Whitehouse died in 1997, interest and knowledge of his work gradually decreased and his writings became virtually forgotten. Recently, the Arthur Jeffery Centre for the Study of Islam, Melbourne School of Theology was handed one of his manuscripts. As a result the Centre began some investigations. That led to a confirmation that Whitehouse was a graduate of the college. In addition, after his retirement from service in the Middle East he became a Lecturer at the College on Islam. In that capacity, he became a forerunner of the Arthur Jeffery Centre with its focus on the study of Islam. A search of the College library revealed that it holds a number of his works.

There is, however, an added dimension to the story. Whitehouse studied Arabic in Egypt under the tutelage of Arthur Jeffery after whom the Centre is named. All this prompted my memory of his Concordance of the Qur'an. In looking at it once again, we realized that this was a valuable resource, that needed to be shared with others.

Getting Whitehouse's work into this format has been both demanding and time-consuming. While seemingly not able to find the original copy of the Arabic Concordance which Whitehouse used, we were able to acquire what appears to be an earlier edition of it. This enabled us to check Whitehouse's work where there were difficulties in transcription. The edition of the Arabic version that we hold includes several introductions as well as a number of lists. Were these in the edition Whitehouse used? We don't know. However, the editorial stance has been to maintain the integrity of the Whitehouse version which we have at our disposal. Some minor changes have been made to the Whitehouse version in order to maintain the logical order of the *suras* and *ayats* (chapters and verses) of the Concordance within a section. Since Whitehouse was a Christian missionary it is not surprising that at the beginning of his work he included a table of the verses in the Qur'an referring to Jesus Christ. That has been retained.

For those for whom a chronological ordering of the Qur'an would be of value, we have chosen to include an outline of the widely accepted Nöldeke's chronology, while recognizing that others have also developed chronologies.

In the spirit of scholarship, we trust that you will find this volume a significant addition to your collection.

Ruth Nicholls
Editor
Arthur Jeffery Centre for the Study of Islam
2018

INTRODUCTION

TO TOPICAL CONCORDANCE TO THE QUR'AN

Although most English translations of the Qur'an are provided with an index, these are generally selective both as to the verses quoted and the subjects dealt with. As a rule, they cover only those subjects which the average non-Muslim reader would consider interesting or important.

However, the serious student of Islam who wants to know something of the way Muslims themselves look at their religion – and more particularly the teaching of the Qur'an – needs something set out within the categories of Muslim theology, philosophy and jurisprudence, and which gives a much wider range of references.

The present brief work is a translation of an Arabic Topical Concordance to the Qur'an produced by the Chief Official Interpreter of Islamic Law (Amin al Fatwa) in Lebanon, Muhammad al Araby al Azuzy, under the title "A Concordance for the Study of Quranic Sciences" published in 1956. He has aimed in the concordance at giving every reference in the Qur'an to the subjects dealt with. The categories used are such as would be used by theologians and jurists in Islam and some of them may therefore seem somewhat strange to non-Muslims. Many of the references used likewise appear vague or indeed irrelevant to those not familiar with the Arabic language or the classical arguments of Muslim theologians. Some will seem far-fetched and fanciful such as a presumed reference in the Qur'an to X-Rays, but perhaps they are not more fanciful than some interpretations of the Bible by some Jewish and Christian expositors.

The compiler of the concordance is a strictly orthodox conservative Muslim and many modern Muslim scholars would not agree that all the references he gives are relevant to the subject. It is hoped however, that this translation will give

5

English students without a knowledge of Arabic, some insight into the conservative Muslim understanding of the teaching of the Qur'an, which, after all, still remains the supreme authority for all Muslims in all matters of religion and, for many, in all matters great and small.

The compiler has set out all the material under the headings used by Muslims, with sub-headings where necessary. Under this he has given every reference to this subject by chapter and verse in order, from chapter one to the end. (In the Arabic original, the names of the chapters are also given but as these are translated in different ways in differing English versions, we have not given these.) The number of the verse as given follows the order of the Arabic Othmani version with the verse number coming at the end and not at the beginning of the verse. As there is no uniformity in numbering (even in the Arabic versions) it may be necessary to refer to two or three verses before and after the number quoted in the concordance if the verse quoted does not appear to have any relevance to the subject. Thus a reference 2:151 might appear in different translations anywhere between say 2:149 and 2:153. For this reason, most English translations which give verse numberings give the number of every 5th verse only. We have checked the translation carefully against the Arabic original, but have not checked the Arabic version itself. This would have been a disproportionate labour and we can assume that the compiler has himself done this most thoroughly.

A. H. Whitehouse
Beirut 1956
AH 1375

Aubrey H. Whitehouse

18 April 1908 - 26 March 1997

Note:
The numbers of the verses given here are the numbers in the official Cairo Arabic version. These numbers may vary as much as four to five verses either way in English translations.

PRINCIPAL QURANIC REFERENCES
(in order)
TO THE CHRIST, JESUS SON OF MARY

Reference	Subject Matter
2:87	Given signs and aided by the Holy Spirit.
2:136	A prophet to whom was given the inspired Gospel.
2:253	Given special proofs of his mission and aided by the Holy Spirit.
3:45-51	Annunciation to Mary of birth of Jesus Christ, Son of Mary, the Word of God, a prophet and worker of miracles.
3:55	Declaration of death and ascension of Jesus.
3:58	Declaration that Jesus, like Adam was created by the Word of God.
3:84	Belief enjoined in the authenticity and authority of the Gospel given to Jesus.
4:154-158	Denial of the death and crucifixion of Christ Jesus Son of Mary.
4:163	Jesus inspired as are all the prophets.
4:171	Christ Jesus, Son of Mary, an apostle of God, the word of God and a spirit from Him. Denial of the possibility of God having a son. Denial of validity of Tri-theism (Trinity).
4:172	Christ does not disdain to be a servant of God.
5:17	Denial that the Messiah the Son of Mary is God. God can destroy Christ Son of Mary and Mary, with all the earth.

5:46	Jesus Son of Mary was given the Gospel of guidance and light, confirming the previous (O.T.) Law. (5:48 – The Qur'an confirms both).
5:72	Christ rebukes the Children of Israel for worshipping Him as God, who is his Lord and theirs.
5:73	The unbelief of declaring "God is the third of three" and the penalty thereof.
5:76	Christ Son of Mary is only a prophet.
5:78	David and Jesus Son of Mary cursed the unbelieving Jews.
5:110	Jesus Son of Mary called on (by God) to remember God's grace to him when he was assisted by the Holy Spirit (Spirit of Holiness) to speak to men from the cradle and perform miracles of creation, healing and raising the dead to life, by the permission of God.
5:111-115	In response to disciples' request and Christ's prayers, a table (of food) descends from Heaven.
5:116-117	Jesus Son of Mary denies that he told the Children of Israel to take him and his mother as two other gods beside God.
6:85	Jesus mentioned as one of God's chosen righteous ones.
9:30-31	Christians rebuked for saying that Christ is Son of God and Lord.
19:16-36	The virgin birth of Christ.
19:30-34	Christ speaks from his cradle, vindicating his mother and declaring God's peace on him on the day of his birth, the day of his resurrection.
19:35-36	Denial that God would take to Himself a son. Assertion by Christ of his being a created being and that God is his Lord.

23:50	The Son of Mary and his mother are made a sign and furnished with security.
33:7	Jesus Son of Mary among the assembled prophets, including Muhammad, from whom God took a rigid compact to declare His truth.
42:13	Jesus, together with Noah, Abraham, Moses and Muhammad inspired and enjoined to be steadfast in religion and avoid becoming divided into sects.
43:57-60	(Jesus) Son of Mary, a servant to whom God has been gracious and a sign to the people of Muhammad.
43:63, 64	Jesus came with manifest signs declaring 'God is my Lord and your Lord.
57:27	Jesus, Son of Mary given the Gospel: kindness and compassion placed in the hearts of his followers.
61:6	Jesus, Son of Mary declares he is apostle of God to the Jews, confirming the Law (O.T.) and prophesying of the advent of another apostle to come after him, Ahmad (Muhammad) by name.
61:14	Believers (Muslims) called on to be the helpers of God as Jesus called on the apostles to be helpers of God.

SECTION 1

THE UNITY (OF GOD)

(a)   Deity and Solitariness:

2:116, 163, 255;

3:6, 18, 62;

4:87, 171;

5:73;

6:19, 102, 106, 164;

7:158;

11:14;

13:30;

14:52;

16:2, 22, 51;

18:38;

20:8, 98;

21:25, 87, 92, 108;

22:34;

27:26, 61, 64;

28:30, 70, 88;

29:46;

35:3;

37:4;

38:65;

39:6;

40:65;

41:6;

43:84;

47:19;

59:22, 23;

64:13;

73:9;

112:1.

(b)   Omnipotence:

2:259;

3:26;

5:17;

6:65, 102;

11:4;

16:40;

25:54;

29:20;

30:54;

35:1, 44;

39:63;

40:68;

42:29;

46:33;

54:55;

57:2;

60:7;

64:1;

65:12;

66:8;

67:1;

70:40;

86:8;

90:5.

(c)   **Calling on God by His Beautiful Names**:
7:180;   **20**:8.
17:11;

(d)   **Knowledge and Omniscience of God:**
2:23, 96, 215, 216, 246, 282;   **34**:2, 3;
3:5;   **35**:38;
6:59, 60, 73, 80;   **36**:76;
7:7;   **39**:8, 46, 70;
10:18;   **40**:2, 19;
11:5, 6, 14, 123;   **41**:47, 54;
12:6, 100;   **42**:12, 25, 51;
13:8, 10, 42;   **43**:84;
14:38;   **47**:19;
15:24;   **48**:4, 26;
16:23, 28, 74;   **49**:13, 16, 18;
17:25, 54, 55;   **50**:4, 16, 45;
18:26, 91;   **51**:30;
19:70;   **53**:30, 32;
20:7, 98, 110;   **57**:3, 4, 6, 10;
21:4, 110;   **58**:3, 7;
22:70, 76;   **59**:22;
23:92, 96;   **64**:4, 8, 11, 18;
24:29, 35, 41, 64;   **65**:12;
25:6, 58;   **66**:2, 3;
27:65, 74, 75, 88, 93;   **68**:7;
28:56;   **72**:26;
29:10, 11, 42, 45, 52, 62;   **76**:30;
30:54;   **87**:7;
31:34;   **90**:7;
32:6;   **100**:11.
33:2, 40, 54;

(e)   **Transcendence of God (above what is not appropriate to Him):**
2:116   **16**:1, 3, 57;
4:40, 171;   **17**:43, 108, 111;
6:100, 102, 136, 144;   **19**:35;
7:54;   **21**:17, 18, 22, 26, 87;
9:31;   **23**:91, 92, 116, 117;
10:18;   **26**:209;
11:101;   **27**:8, 61, 64;
14:30;   **30**:9;

36:83;
37:159, 180;
39:4, 5, 66, 67;
40:64;
43:15, 16, 76, 81, 82;
50:29, 38;

52:43;
55:78;
59:23;
69:52;
87:1;
112:3, 4.

(f) **The Attributes of God (such as knowledge, life, power, will, etc.):**

1:1-4;
2:106, 107, 117, 120, 128, 137, 138, 158, 163, 186, 207, 209, 213, 216, 234, 235, 253, 255, 267, 284;
3:2, 31, 54, 109, 129, 135, 156, 189;
4:43, 85, 92, 96, 99, 100, 108, 110, 122, 129, 130, 132, 135, 152, 173;
5:1, 7, 8, 17, 18, 38, 40, 54, 64, 76, 95, 97, 101, 105, 109, 114, 116, 117, 120;
6:3, 12, 14, 17, 18, 54, 57, 62, 72, 73, 80, 95, 96, 101, 102, 103, 108, 115, 117, 128, 132, 139, 145, 146, 164, 165;
7:54, 57, 89, 158, 180;
8:10, 13, 17, 25, 29, 30, 41, 44, 48, 49, 51, 53, 61, 63, 69, 70, 75;
9:5, 15, 16, 27, 28, 39, 40, 60, 71, 78, 91, 97, 99, 102, 106, 110, 115, 118, 129;
10:31, 32, 36, 55, 56, 65, 68, 107, 109;
11:4, 5, 123;
12:34, 64, 80, 100;
13:2, 6, 13, 14, 16, 30, 31, 33, 40, 41;
14:1, 2, 4, 8, 10, 20, 32, 47, 48, 51, 52;
15:22, 23, 49, 50, 86;
16:9, 12, 17, 19, 47, 52, 60, 77, 110, 115, 125;
17:1, 17, 30, 66, 96;
18:26, 58;
19:40, 65;
20:6, 52, 73, 98, 110, 114;
21:4, 19, 23;
22:6, 10, 14, 18, 40, 41, 52, 56, 59, 64, 74;
23:14, 80, 84, 89, 116;
24:21, 22, 25, 28, 30, 33, 35, 41, 42, 58, 60, 62, 64;
25:2, 6, 20, 70;
26:9, 68, 104, 122, 140, 159, 175, 191, 220;
28:58, 70;
29:5, 42, 60;

15

30:5, 27;
31:12, 16, 23, 26, 30, 34;
32:2-5;
33:1-5, 17, 19, 25, 27, 34, 38, 50, 52, 59, 73;
34:3, 11, 23, 47, 48, 50;
35:2, 10, 13, 15, 28, 41;
36:5, 38, 79, 83;
38:65, 66;
39:37, 45, 62, 63;
40:2-3, 12, 15, 16, 20, 22, 56, 65;
41:12, 32, 39, 43, 54;
42:3-5, 9, 11, 12, 19, 23, 24, 27, 28, 49, 50, 51;
43:9, 85;
44:6-8;
45:2, 27, 36, 37;
46:2;
47:38;
48:11, 14, 24;
49: 1, 5, 12;
50:29, 43, 45;
53:31, 43, 45;

55: 1, 29, 78;
57:1-2, 4-6, 9, 24, 28, 29;
58:1-3, 6-7, 11, 13, 21;
59:1, 6-7, 22, 24;
60:3, 5, 7, 12;
61:1;
62:1;
64:2, 6-7, 14, 18;
66:1;
67:1-2, 19;
70:40;
78:37;
82:19;
85:14, 16;
92:12,13;
112:2.

(g)   God's Purpose (Will) in His Creation:

2:210, 253;
6:107, 112, 133, 148;
9:106;
10:99, 100;
11:118, 119;
14:11, 27;
16:93;
17:54, 86;
29:21;
32:13;

35:16, 17;
36:66, 67;
42:8, 24, 49, 50;
43:33, 35, 60;
48:14, 25;
64:2;
65:3;
74:56;
76:30;
81:29.

(h)   The Miracles (Signs) of God and the Infidelity of Those Who Deny Them:

2:164, 242, 252;
6:65, 105, 109, 126;
7:32, 35, 58, 146, 147;
10:5-6, 15, 20, 67;

12:105,
13:2, 4;
16:11, 12, 67, 69, 79;
17:1, 41, 59;

18:105;
19:77;
23:30;
24;18, 46, 58, 59;
26:8, 67, 121, 139 ,158, 174, 190;
27:52, 82, 86, 93;
28:71, 73;
29:15;
30:20, 27, 37, 46, 58;
31: 31, 32;
32:15, 26;

33:34;
34:9, 19;
39:42, 53, 64;
40:13, 81;
41:37, 39;
42:15, 29, 32;
45:3-9, 11,13;
51:20, 21;
53:55, 58, 60;
57:17.

SECTION 2

FAITH
(Articles of Belief)

(a)   Belief in God:

2:62, 136, 137, 177, 256, 285;	**27:**81;
3:84, 110, 162;	**42:**13;
4:39, 59, 136, 171;	**48:**9;
5:111;	**57:**7;
7:156, 158;	**61:**11;
9:18, 19, 44;	**64:**8, 11;
23:58;	**67:**29.

(b)   Belief – in Angels:
2:97, 98, 177, 285.

(c)   Belief – in the Books:

2:4, 41, 89, 91, 97, 136, 177,	**7:**158;
285;	**35:**25;
3:65, 84;	**42:**13.
4:47, 136, 162;	

(d)   Belief – in Prophets and Messengers:

2:98, 136, 137, 177, 253, 285;	**10:**103;
3:84;	**17:**15, 55;
4:64, 136, 150, 171;	**18:**106;
5:12, 22, 99, 109, 111;	**21:**6-9;
6:34, 86, 87, 89, 130;	**42:**13.
7:53;	

(e)   Belief – in Last Day and the Unbelief of Those Who Deny it:

2:4, 46, 62, 123, 177;	**10:**45;
3:9, 25;	**16:**22;
4:38, 39, 59, 162;	**27:**3;
6:113;	**31:**4;
7:147;	**42:**7;
9:18, 19, 44;	**70:**26.

(f)   Belief – in Predestination - to Good and Evil:

6:17, 18, 27;   **13:**11.
10:19;

(g)   Belief – in the Unseen:

2:3;   **16:**77;
6:59;   **36:**11.
10:20;

(h)   Belief – the Old Testament (Torah):

3:3, 48, 50, 65, 93;   **9:**111;
5:43, 44, 46, 110;   **17:**4.

(i)   Belief – the New Testament (Gospel – Injeel):

3:3, 48, 65;   **9:**111;
5:46, 47, 110;   **57:**27.

(j)   Belief – the Psalms (Zubur):

4:163;   **21:**105;
17:55;   **35:**25.

(k)   Belief in the Qur'an:

2:2, 41, 97, 99, 129, 137, 176,   **21:**50,
185;   **22:**54;
3:4, 7, 84;   **24:**1;
4:136, 140, 162;   **25:**1, 6;
5:15, 48;   **26:**195, 210, 211;
6:153, 157;   **32:**2;
7:2-3, 52;   **34:**6, 49;
8:41;   **36:**2, 5, 11;
9:111;   **38:**86, 88;
10:16, 40, 57, 108;   **39:**1-2, 28, 42,56;
11:1, 17;   **40:**2;
12:2, 104;   **41:**2-3, 42, 44;
13:1, 19, 37;   **42:**7, 17;
14:1;   **43:**2, 4;
15:1, 9, 87;   **44:**2, 4;
16:103;   **45:**2;
17:105, 107;   **46:**2, 12;
18:1;   **50:**1;
20:113;   **52:**2, 3;

53:3-4;   74:54;
56:77, 80;   80:12, 16;
59:21;   81:19;
64:8;   85:21, 22;
65:10;   86:13, 14;
69:40, 43, 51;   97:1.

(l)   Information in the Qur'an about the Past and Future (of inventions such as air planes and what it means):
6:65, 125;   17:12, 89;
16:8;   38:1.

(m)   The Inimitability of the Qur'an:
2:23;   14:52;
4:82;   17:88;
10:38;   31:27;
11:13;   38:88.
13:31;

(n)   Its Embracing Knowledge of First Things and Last Things:
2:41, 97, 151;   18:54;
3:3;   20:113;
5:101;   30:58;
6:38, 65, 92   31:27;
12:111;   35:31;
16:89;   39:28.

(o)   Confirmation of the Qur'an of the Previous Heavenly
        Scriptures and the Abrogation of Them:
4:47;   10:37;
5:48;   46:12.

(p)   Abrogation of Certain Verses by Others:
2:100;   16:101;
13:39;   22:52.

(q)   The Plain (Verses) and the Ambiguous:
3:7;   39:24, 56.

(r)   The Safeguarding of the Qur'an from Alteration or
Substitution:
2:181;   6:115;

15:9.

(s)   The Infidelity of Those Who Believe Part of it and Deny Other Parts:

13:36;   **15:**91.

(t)   The Arrangement of the Qur'an (Its revelation in stages, the ease of memorizing it and the duty of listening to it):

2:121, 185, 242, 252;   **26:**2;
3:58, 108, 138;   **27:**1;
4:82;   **28:**2;
6:55, 114;   **29:**49;
7:52, 53, 204;   **31:**2;
8:2;   **35:**29;
9:11, 124, 127;   **38:**29;
10:1;   **39:**23;
11:1, 120;   **41:**3;
12:1;   **47:**24;
13:1;   **54:**17, 22, 32, 40;
15:1;   **56:**79;
16:98;   **57:**16;
17:45, 78, 107, 109;   **73:**4, 20.
19:97;

(u)   The Duty of Repeating (reciting) it, its guidance to man, and the sanctity of hiding it (in the heart):

2:2, 97, 159, 174, 176;   **32:**22;
4:37;   **34:**6;
5:16;   **37:**13;
6:70;   **38:**1, 29, 87;
7:2, 26, 52;   **41:**4, 44;
10:57;   **42:**52;
12:104, 111;   **45:**11, 20;
13:30;   **50:**45;
14:52;   **52:**29;
16:64, 89, 102;   **59:**21;
17:9, 41;   **68:**52;
22:16;   **69:**48;
24:34;   **74:**55;
25:50, 73;   **76:**29;
27:2, 77;   **80:**12, 13,
31:3;   **81:**27, 28.

(v)   The Infidelity of Those Who Deride it and Deny (its validity):

2:170, 171, 231;

3:19, 72;

4:51, 140;

5:44;

6:5, 7, 25, 33, 57, 66, 68;

7:9;

8:31;

9:65;

10:15, 17, 37, 38, 39, 94;

13:1;

16:24, 103, 104;

17:41, 47, 48, 89;

18:56, 57, 101, 106;

19:73, 77;

20:100, 101, 126;

21:2, 24, 32, 50;

22:51, 55, 57, 72;

23:63, 105;

25:4-5, 30, 50;

29:23, 47, 49, 68;

30:10;

32:22;

34:5, 43;

37:12, 14;

39:57;

40:4, 81;

41:40, 41;

43:36;

45:35;

77:50;

81:25;

90:19.

(w)   Testing and Warning Believers:

2:104, 155;

3:30, 100, 101, 118, 141, 144, 149, 152, 154, 156, 166, 186, 195;

5:48;

6:53, 54, 108;

8:5, 17, 21, 47;

9:16, 122;

10:32;

11:7, 113;

29:2-3;

32:18;

33:11, 69;

47:31, 38;

60:6;

63:9;

67:2.

(x)   Glad Tidings for Believers and Believers' Qualities:

2: 25, 82, 105, 112, 143, 165, 177, 207, 218, 257, 277;

3:30, 57, 68, 73, 74, 103, 107, 126, 136, 139, 140, 154, 163, 164, 172, 174, 179, 195;

4:57, 69, 70, 79, 115, 122, 124, 136, 141, 146, 147, 152, 162, 173, 175;

5:9, 35, 54, 59, 69, 93, 94, 105, 119;

6:16, 36, 48, 51, 52, 82, 92, 97, 127;

7:10, 49;

8:1, 4, 7, 11, 19, 40, 41, 62, 63, 72, 74, 75;

9:20, 21, 71, 72, 88, 89, 99, 111, 112, 120, 124;

10:3, 9, 25, 26, 58, 63, 64, 103;
11:11, 23;
12:57;
13:18, 21, 22, 28, 29;
14:11, 14, 23, 27;
16:32;
17:9, 107,109;
18:2-3, 30, 31, 107, 108;
19:60, 63, 72, 76, 96;
20:75, 112;
21:94, 101, 105,106;
22:14, 23, 24, 31, 34, 35, 37, 41, 50, 54, 56;
23:1, 11, 57, 61, 109, 111;
24:37, 38, 51, 55, 62;
25:24, 63, 64, 67, 68, 73, 76;
26:227;
27:3, 62;
28:67;
29:7, 9, 51, 58, 69;
30:15, 38, 45;
31:3, 5, 8;
32:15, 17, 19;
33:22, 23, 35, 47, 70, 71, 73;
34:4, 37;
35:7, 18, 29, 30;
36:11;
37:40, 49, 74, 160;
38:24, 28;
39:10, 17, 74, 75;
40:7, 9, 51;
41:8, 30, 32;
42:22, 23, 26, 36, 37;
43:68, 73;
45:21, 30;

46:13, 14, 16, 19;
47:2, 3, 5, 7, 12, 17;
48:4, 5, 9, 26, 29;
50:32, 33;
51:15, 19;
52:21, 22;
56:10, 24, 27, 40;
57:12, 14, 16, 19;
58:22;
59:8, 18;
60:4, 6, 7;
61:10, 11;
64:9;
65:11;
66:8;
67:12;
69:19, 24;
70:22, 27, 29, 30, 32, 35;
74:39, 40;
75:22;
76:5, 9;
79:45;
82:13;
83:18, 28;
84:25;
85:11;
87:14, 15;
89:27, 30;
92:17, 21;
95:6;
98:7, 8;
103:3.

(y)   Islam – Following it and Death as a Muslim in it:
2:112;
3:19, 20, 102;
4:125;
5:3;
6:14, 71, 125, 163;

8:38;
9:11;
11:14;
21:92, 108;
22:78;

29:46;
30:43;
33:35;
39:23;

42:13;
43:69;
46:15.

SECTION 3

TAKING REFUGE (IN GOD)

(a)   **Taking Refuge in God and Trusting Him**

1:5;	**29:**59;
3:101, 103, 159, 173;	**30:**33;
4:146, 175;	**31:**22;
5:23;	**33:**3;
8:2, 49;	**39:**38;
9:51, 116;	**40:**44;
11:123;	**42:**10, 36;
13:30;	**58:**10;
14:11, 12;	**64:**13;
16:42;	**65:**3;
17:45, 46;	**67:**29.
22:78;	

(b)   **Praiseworthiness of Unity and the Evil of Divisions**

3:103, 105, 152;	**9:**107;
8:43, 46;	**30:**32.

SECTION 4

PURITY

(a)   **Purity of Body and Clothing:**
4:43;   **74:**4.
9:108;

(b)   **Purity of Water:**
25:48.

(c)   **Need for "Washing" (gusl) :**
4:43;   **9:**28.
5:6;

(d)   **Ceremonial Purification (wudu') and its Regulations:**
4:43;   **25:**48.
5:6;

(e)   **Purification with Sand (tayummum) and its Regulations:**
4:43;   **5:**6.

(f)   **Menstruation and Confinement and Regulations:**
2:222;   **13:**8, 9.

SECTION 5

PRAYER

(a)   Sacrament of Prayer and Submission in it:

2:3, 43, 177;	**30:**18;
4:77;	**31:**4, 17;
5:12 ,55;	**38:**33, 56;
6:162;	**35:**18, 29;
7: 26,27;	**39:**1;
9:112;	**42:**38;
17:78, 110;	**48:**29;
20:121;	**58:**13;
21:73;	**70:**22, 23;
22:41, 77, 78;	**73:**20;
23:1-2;	**74:**3;
24:37, 56;	**96:**1;
27:3;	**98:**5;
29:45;	**107:**4-6.

(b)   Times of Prayer and the Call to it:

5:58;	**41:**33;
17:78;	**62:**9.
20:130;	

(c)   The Qibla (Direction of Prayer) and Regulations Concerning it:

2:115, 142, 145, 147, 150;   **7:**29.

(d)   Mosques (Places of worship), Regulations and Retirement to Them:

2:114, 144, 149, 187;	**17:**1;
4:43;	**21:**71;
7:29, 31;	**22:**25;
8:34;	**24:**36;
9:17, 19, 28, 107, 110;	**72:**18.

(e)   Observance of Prayer (intercessory prayer and the "Dhikr" following it):

2:45, 110, 153, 177, 238;   **4:**103, 162;

5:91;   18:46;
6:72, 92;   19:59;
8:3;   20:14, 130, 132;
9:5, 11, 18, 71   23:9;
11:114;   29:45;
13:22;   30:17, 31;
14:31;   70:23, 34.

(f)   Prayer at the Two Feasts:
108:2.

(g)   Friday Prayers:
62:9, 11;   **85:**3.

(h)   Prayer on a Journey:
4:101.

(i)   The Prayer of Fear:
2:239;   **4:**101, 102.

(j)   Spending the Night in Prayer and Voluntary (Prayer):
6:162;   **25:**64;
11:114;   **32:**16;
17:79;   **15:**17, 18.

(k)   Worship and Reciting (The Qur'an):
7:206;   **27:**26;
13:15;   **32:**15;
16:49;   **38:**24;
17:109;   **41:**38;
19:58;   **53:**62;
22:18, 77;   **84:**21;
25:60;   **96:**19.

**(l)   What is Forbidden in Prayer and Prohibition of Prayer to Other
           Than God:**
2:34;   **32:**15;
4:43;   **41:**37;
16:48, 49;   **77:**48.
22:18;

SECTION 6

(LEGAL) ALMSGIVING (ZAKAT)

(a)   The Obligation of it and Giving of it Freely:

2:43, 110, 177;   31:4;
4:77, 162;   33:33;
5:12, 55;   35:18;
6:141, 143;   41:7;
7:156;   51:19;
9:5, 11, 18, 60, 103;   57:7;
21:73;   58:13;
22:41, 78;   70:24;
23:4, 60;   73:20;
24:37, 56;   92:18;
27:3;   98:5;
30:39;   107:7.

(b)   What is Subject and Exempt from Almsgiving:

9:60, 103, 104;   70:24, 25.

SECTION 7

FASTING

(a)   Duty (of Fasting) and Preparation for it:
2:183, 185.

(b)   Exemption from Fasting and What is Lawful for the One Fasting:
2:184, 185, 187.

(c)   God's Provision (Reward) for Fasting etc.:
9:112;   **97:**2, 5.
44:4, 6;

SECTION 8

PILGRIMAGE

(a)   Duty of Pilgrimage:
2:125, 128, 158, 197, 198,   **9:**3;
      199, 200, 203;   **22:**28, 29, 30, 33;
3:97;   **85:**3.
5:3;
6:162;

(b)   Compensation, Offerings and Rules for Same:
2:196;   **22:**28, 32, 34, 36, 37;
5:2, 97;   **48:**25.

(c)   What Maybe Enjoyed and What is Restricted:
2:196;   **5:**2.

(d)   What is Forbidden to the Pilgrim:
2:197.

(e)   Trading During the Pilgrimage:
2:197;   **22:**28.

(f)   Providing Water for Pilgrims:
9:19.

(g)   Law of Hunting During Pilgrimage:
5:1, 2, 95, 96.

(h)   Completion of Pilgrimage and the Minor Pilgrimage:
2:196;   **22:**29;
5:2;   **47:**27.

(i)   The "House", The Kaaba and "The Mosque":
2:125, 127;   **8:**34, 35;
3:96, 97;   **9:**7, 19, 28;
5:2, 97;   **17:**1;
6:123;   **22:**25, 33;

27:91;   **52**:4.
42:7;

SECTION 9

MARRIAGE

(a)   **Marriage – Rules and Regulations, Engagement:**

2:222, 223, 235;
4:3, 4, 20, 21, 24 ,25;
5:5;
16:72;
23:6;
24:26, 32, 60;
28:27;

30:21;
33:49, 50;
35:11;
42:11, 49, 50;
60:10;
70:30.

(b)   **Conjugal Rights of Marriage Partners and Justice Between them:**

4:3, 19, 129;
38:44.

(c)   **Marriage of Orphans:**

4:3, 24, 25, 36, 128;
5:5;
23:6;

24:32;
33:50.

(d)   **Laws Concerning Marriage with "Unbelieving" Women:**

2:221;
4:22, 23, 24.

(e)   **Judgment Between Marriage Partners on Separation:**

4:35, 128;
58:1.

(f)   **Abstinence from Marriage:**

24:33ff.

(g)   **Expectations from Marriage:**

16:72;
24:32.

(h)   **Separation and Marital Discord:**

2:232;
4:19, 34, 128.

SECTION 10

DIVORCE

(a)   Divorce – Regulations:
2:227, 229, 232, 240, 241;   **65:**1,2;
4:130;   **66:**1.

(b)   Prohibition Against Force etc.:
2:231, 236, 237;   **65:**1, 6.
33:49;

(c)   Divorce with Wife's Consent:
2:229;   **4:**19.

(d)   Necessity of Separation of Infidel from His Wife if She becomes a Muslim:
60:10, 11.

(e)   Number of Divorces and Dowry:
2: 228, 231;   **65:**1, 2, 4, 6.

(f)   Compensation After Divorce etc.:
2:234, 236, 241;   **33:**49.

(g)   Sundry Laws About Divorce, Adoption, Weaning, etc.:
2:226, 227, 233;   **46:**15;
31:14;   **58:**1, 4;
33:4, 5, 40;   **65:**6.

SECTION 11

LIVING EXPENSES

2:215, 233, 280;   **65:**6, 7.
17:26;

SECTION 12

OATHS and COVENANTS

(a)   **Swearing and Necessity of Performing Oaths:**
2:224, 225;   **38:**44;
16:91, 92, 94;   **68:**10.
24:22;

(b)   **Expiation of Oaths and Invalidating of Them:**
2:225;   **66:**2.
5:89;

(c)   **Vows and Their Laws:**
2:270;   **22:**29;
3:35;   **76:**7.

SECTION 13

BUYING and SELLING

(a)   Trading and Profit:

2:282;

4:29;

5:1;

24:37;

28:73;

29:17;

30:23;

35:29; 30;

38:24.

(b)   Weights and Measures:

6:152;

11:84, 85;

17:35;

55:7, 9;

83:1, 3.

(c)   Trade on Land and Sea etc.:

2:164, 188, 267, 275;

3:77;

4:2, 29, 161;

5:42, 62, 63, 100;

7:10;

15:20, 21;

16:14;

17:66, 70;

18:77, 94;

28:25;

30:46;

35:12;

45:12;

67:15.

(d)   Bankruptcy, Partnership etc.:

2:177;

4:5, 6, 32;

6:165;

13:26;

16:71;

17:21, 30, 34;

24:33, 38;

34:36, 39;

39:53;

42:12, 27;

43:32.

(e)   **The Duty of Putting Loans in Writing etc.:**
2:282, 283;   **5:**1;
4:6;   **28:**26, 29.

(f)   **Laws about Usury:**
2:275, 276, 278, 279;   **4:**161;
3:130;   **30:**39.

SECTION 14

FARMING

2:266, 267;   **21:**78;
6:95, 99, 141;   **56:**63, 64, 65.
7:58;

SECTION 15

CONJUGAL RIGHTS and INHERITANCE

2:180, 182, 220, 240;
4:2, 7, 8, 10, 11, 12, 13, 19, 32, 33, 127, 176;
5:106;   **17:**34;
6:152;   **33:**6.
8:75, 83;

SECTION 16

CALIPHATE and EMIRATE

(a)   Administration of the State:

20:29;   40:26, 28;
24:62;   42:38;
27:32, 34, 37;   59:7.
28:34;

(b)   Allegiance and Obedience to Caliph:

2:30;   35:39;
4:59, 83;   38:26;
6:165;   39:75;
10:14;   60:12, 75;
24:55;   64:16.
27:28, 31, 36, 62;

SECTION 17

JUSTICE, WITNESS (TESTIMONY) ETC.

(a)   Judgment between Men by the Qur'an (justice: prohibition of bribery, oppression):

2:188, 213;	**33:**2, 36;
3:23;	**38:**22, 26;
4:58, 59, 61, 83, 85, 105, 135;	**39:**70, 76;
5:8, 42, 44, 45, 47, 50;	**42:**10, 13, 15, 17;
6:57, 114, 152;	**47:**22, 23;
7:29;	**49:**9;
16:76, 90, 95;	**55:**7, 8;
21:78;	**75:**25;
27:32;	**60:**10, 11.

(b)   Punishment: Capital Punishment, Wrong of Suicide:

2:178, 179;	**16:**126;
4:29, 92, 93;	**17:**33;
5:32, 33, 45;	**22:**60;
6:151;	**25:**68.

(c)   Compensation to Victim's Family (if a "believer"):

4:92;	**17:**33.

(d)   Witness and Witnesses: True and False:

2:42, 140, 143, 146, 147, 283, 284;

3:29;	**24:**21;
4:135;	**43:**19;
5:8, 44, 106, 108;	**49:**6;
6:152;	**70:**33; (false witness)
12:81;	**24:**4, 5;
17:36;	**25:**72.

(e)   Prohibition of Defamation:

2:204;	**41:**34;
21:18;	**67:**21;
36:77;	**68:**13.

(f)   Adultery, Its Penalty and Testimony to:

4:15, 16, 19, 24, 25;   24:2, 3, 26, 33;

17:32;   25:68.

23:5;

(g)   Theft, Cursing and Their Punishment:

5:38;   24:6.

(h)   Defamation and Its Penalty:

24:4, 6, 9, 23.

(i)   Duty of Submission to God's Judgment:

4:65;   33:36;

5:2, 87, 94;   58:4,5;

9:112;   59:7;

23:7;   65:1, 5;

24:63;   70:31.

25:68, 69;

(j)   Sodomy and Lesbianism and Penalty:

4:16;   27: 54, 55;

26:165, 166;   29:28, 29.

SECTION 18

FOOD, DRINK, HUNTING, ETC

(a)   Purpose of Eating and Drinking and "Saying Grace":

2:168, 172;   **20:**54;
5:4, 5, 87, 88, 93;   **23:**19, 21;
6:141, 142, 145;   **24:**61;
7:31, 32, 160;   **36:**33, 36;
8:26;   **40:**64;
16:5, 10, 11, 14, 66, 69, 114;   **76:**5, 17, 21.

(b)   Permitted (Lawful) Food and Drink:

2:173, 219;   **6:**121, 145;
4:43;   **16:**115.
5:3, 90;

(c)   Lawful and Unlawful Hunting on Land and Sea:

2:173, 219;   **6:**121, 145;
4:43;   **16:**14, 115;
5:1, 2, 3, 4, 90, 94, 96;   **35:**12.

(d)   What is Essential and Unlawful in Slaughtering:

2:173;   **16:**115;
5:1, 3, 4;   **22:**30, 34, 36.
6:118, 119, 121, 145;

SECTION 19

CLOTHING and ORNAMENTS

7:26, 31, 32;
16:5, 14, 81;
18:31;

22:23;
43:18;
76:15, 16, 21.

SECTION 20

MEDICINE and ANATOMY

2:243, 275;
7:200, 201;
10:57;
16:69;
17:82;

25:67;
26:80;
41:44;
75:4, 27.

SECTION 21

VISIONS and THEIR INTERPRETATION

12:3, 6, 36, 41, 43 ,49, 100,
101;
17:60;

37:102, 105;
48:27.

SECTION 22

JIHAD (HOLY WAR)

(a)   Duty of/and Religious Freedom:

2:190, 194, 216, 244, 256;	**17:**54;
4:74, 77, 84, 89, 91, 94;	**22:**39, 78;
5:35, 54;	**42:**39, 41, 42;
8:39, 40, 65, 74, 75;	**47:**4;
9:5, 6, 12, 14, 19, 29, 123;	**61:**4, 14;
10:99;	**66:**9.

(b)   Mobilization and the Law of War in the Sacred Months:

2:194, 217;	**8:**5;
4:71, 84, 95;	**9:**5, 36, 39, 41, 42, 81.
5:2, 97;	

(c)   Laws of Martyrdom and What God has Prepared for Martyrs:

2:154;	**9:**82, 111;
3:157, 158, 169, 172, 195;	**57:**19;
4:95, 96;	**61:**12.
8:6;	

(d)   Preparations, Military and Economic Against the Enemy:

2:195, 245;	**16:**81;
3:200;	**21:**80;
4:95, 102;	**55:**35;
6:65;	**57:**25;
8:60;	**64:**17.
9:46;	

(e)   Obligation of Holy War on Person and Possessions:

2:207, 262;	**49:**15;
8:60, 72;	**57:**7, 10, 11;
9:20, 41, 44, 53, 81, 88, 111, 121;	**61:**11.

(f)   Poll Tax, Prisoners and Redemption:

8:67, 70;	**9:**29;

47:4;   90:13.

(g)   Battle Array and Steadfastness in Battle:
2:177, 249;   8:15, 16, 45, 46, 66;
3:121, 122, 125, 146, 147,   9:25, 112, 123;
    155;   16:110.
4:104;

(h)   Laws Against those who Refuse to Fight:
2:195;
9:13, 24, 38, 42, 46, 81, 87, 90, 92, 96, 101, 103, 104, 106, 118, 120;
23:21;
48:11, 12, 15, 16.

(i)   Spying
2:27;   9:3, 9, 12;
4:91;   49:9, 10, 12.

(j)   Victory to Believers – Angelic Assistance:
2:214;   9:26, 51;
8:12, 66;   22:39, 40.

(k)   Fear of God in Hearts of Infidels:
2:137, 214;
3:13, 111, 126, 127, 147, 150, 152, 160;
4:45, 84;   33:9, 10;
6:34;   37:137;
8:10, 14, 18, 19, 26, 36, 65,   40:4;
    66;   42:39;
9:14, 15, 25, 111;   47:7, 35;
12:110;   48:18, 29;
13:42;   58:22;
14:14;   61:13.
22:39, 40;
30:47;

(l)   Armistice, Peace and Surrender:
2:208, 210;   9:1, 2, 4;
4:90, 91, 94;   47:35;
8:61, 62, 72;   49:9.

(m)   **Spoil and its Division:**

3:161;

4:94;

8:1, 41, 69;

48:19, 21;

59:7.

(n)   **Judgments Concerning Weaklings and those who Make Excuses:**

2:273;

4:75, 95, 97, 98, 99;

9:90, 92;

48:17, 25.

(o)   **Various Judgments Concerning Flight:**

2:218;

3:195;

4:97, 100;

8:71, 72, 74, 75;

9:20;

16:41, 110;

25:40, 58, 59;

29:56;

33:50;

39:11;

59:8;

60:10, 12.

SECTION 23

VERITIES and VIRTUES

(a)   Good Intentions and Sincerity in Work:

2:286;   31:22;
3:145, 148;   39:2, 3, 11, 14;
9:105, 109;   40:14, 65;
13:11;   41:6;
22:11;   42:26.
30:30;

(b)   Fear and Reverence for God:

1:1, 5;   31:33;
2:74, 150;   33:39;
3:31;   36:11;
4:9, 77, 108;   39:16, 23;
5:3, 44, 54, 94;   59:21;
6:45;   67:12;
9:13, 18;   76:10;
22:35;   79:40, 41;
23:57;   98:8.
24:52;

(c)   Worship and Obedience to God:

1:5;   30:18, 26;
2:21, 22, 73, 172;   33:33, 36, 71;
3:22, 64, 132;   36:61;
4:1, 13, 36, 59, 69;   39:9;
5:92;   40:65;
8:1, 20, 24, 46;   47:33;
9:31, 71;   48:17;
10:3, 104;   51:56, 57;
11:2, 123;   53:62;
21:92;   58:13;
22:11, 26, 77, 78;   64:12;
24:52, 56;   98:5.
29:56;

(d)   Goodness of God to His Servants:

2: 268;

10:66;

11:3;

19:93, 95;

22:18;

24:10, 20, 21;

27:73;

32:4, 43;

35:2;

39:44, 53;

40:3, 61;

41:22;

42:19, 25, 30;

45:13;

48:29;

53:32;

57:29;

59:10;

60:12;

62:4;

67:14, 15;

73:20;

78:36.

(e)   Remonstrance of God Against Mankind:

2:28;

4:165;

6:37, 40, 149;

10:29, 31, 34, 35, 61;

17:99;

23:84, 90;

27:60;

31:25;

34:9, 24, 48;

36:71, 78, 83;

39:38;

40:50, 57, 63;

43:78, 87;

45:31;

46:4;

56:57, 73;

67:19;

75:3, 6, 36, 40;

77:50;

80:24, 32;

89:5;

95:7.

(f)   God's Appointment of His Apostle to the Believers:

2:257;

5:55;

7:155, 196;

8:34;

10:62;

47:11.

(g)   Charity and the Charitable:

2:112, 245, 286;

5:93;

7:42, 56;

9:120, 121;

10:26;

11:115;

12:56;

16:30, 90;

21:94;

23:62;

29:69;

51:16;

55:60;

60:7.

(h)   Guidance of God (Are believers and unbelievers equal?):

1:1, 7;

2:38, 213, 272;

6:35, 39, 71, 88, 125, 144, 149;

7 :30, 155, 178, 186;

9:18, 19, 37, 80, 115;

10:25, 35, 74, 108;

16:9, 36, 37 ,64, 93, 104, 107;

17:97;

18:17, 29, 57;

20:50;

22:54;

24:46;

25:31, 42;

27:63, 92;

28:85;

30:29, 53;

32:13;

33:4;

35:8, 19, 22, 45;

36:62;

39:18, 19, 23, 37, 38, 42;

4:131, 175;

5:105;

13:27, 33;

14:4, 10, 13, 21, 27;

40:33, 58;

42:13, 44, 46;

43:40;

45:23;

46:10;

48:20;

59:20;

67:22;

68:6, 7, 35, 36;

74:31;

76:31;

80:2, 4;

87:3;

92:12, 15, 16

(i)   Repentance and its Conditions:

2:160;

3:89, 135;

4:16, 18, 146;

9:5, 15, 27, 104, 112, 117, 118;

11:3;

13:30;

16:119;

19:60;

20:82;

24:5, 22, 31;

25:70, 71;

28:67;

5:34, 39, 74;

6:54;

30:31;

39:45;

40:3;

42:25;

46:15;

58:13;

66:8

(j)   Godliness and the Godly:

2:177, 189, 194, 196, 197. 202, 206, 212, 281;

3:76, 102, 130, 198, 200;

4:9, 131;

5:2, 4, 7, 8, 58, 88, 93, 96, 100, 108, 112;
6:32, 69, 72, 155;
7:26, 35, 156, 201;
8:1, 29, 34, 69;
9:4, 36, 44, 119;
10:6, 63;
11:49;
12:109;
13:35;
15:45, 48;
16:2, 30, 31, 52, 128;
39: 11, 17, 21, 34, 35, 62, 74;
43:35, 67;
44:51, 53;
45:19;
47:36;
49:10, 12, 13;
50:31;
51:15, 16;
52:17;
54:54, 55;

19:85;
20:132;
21:48, 49;
24:52;
25:15, 16;
28:83;
30:31;
32:31;
33:55, 70;
38:28, 49, 54;

58:9;
59:7, 18;
60:11;
64:16;
65:2, 3 ,4, 5, 10;
68:34;
74:56;
77:41, 44;
78:31, 36

.

(k)   **Good and Evil: Harmful and Useful:**
2:212,
6:17,
10:107
11:6;
16:17, 53, 54, 72, 83;
20:132;
27:64;
29:60, 62;
30:37, 40;

34:24 ,36 ,39;
39:37, 39;
42:19, 27, 30;
51:5, 22, 23, 57, 58;
53:48;
57:22, 23;
64:11;
67:21.

(l)   **God's Commands to Man:**
31:14, 15, 20;
33:43;
36:77 ,80;
39:7, 8;
43:10, 13;
49:1;

57:25;
59:19;
66:6;
86:5, 7;
90:8, 10.

SECTION 24

ETHICAL CONDUCT

(a)   Every Man Responsible for His Works:

2:26, 110, 281, 286;   39:8, 42;
6:164;   40:17, 40;
10:4;   41:46;
11:109, 111, 123;   42:30;
14:51;   45:15, 22;
16:97;   52:21;
17:13, 15, 19, 84;   53:31, 38, 41;
18:46;   73:20;
20:112;   74:38;
21:47;   76:3, 29;
29:6;   84:6;
30:44;   89:14;
32:17;   92:4;
35:18;   99:7, 8.
36:12;

(b)   Desires to Spend Money (What is lawful and Concealing Almsgiving):

2:3, 177, 215 ,219, 254, 261, 262, 265, 267, 270, 272, 274, 276;
3:17, 92, 134;   32:16;
4:39, 40;   34:39;
5:12;   35:29;
8:3;   42:38;
9:34;   47:36, 38;
13:22;   51:19;
14:31;   57:7, 18;
16:75;   63:10;
17:100;   64:16;
24:22;   73:20;
25:67;   92:18, 20.

(c)   Instinctive Habits, Patience, Goodwill and Truthfulness:

2:45, 138, 153, 155, 157, 177, 249;
3:17, 165, 186, 200;
8:46;
9:119;
11:11;
13:22, 24;
14:5, 12;
16:43 ,96, 126, 127;

19:65;
28:80;
29:10, 59;
31:17, 31;
33:8;
39:10;
42:43;
64:11.

(d)   Rights of Friendship, Hospitality and Co-operation:

4:36
5:2;
7:43
11:78;
24:61;

25:28, 29;
43:67;
76:8, 9;
90:14, 16.

(e)   Guardianship of Women by Men and Duty of Women Veiling:

4:24, 34;
24:27, 31, 58, 60, 62;
32:33;

33:53, 55, 59;
70:29.

(f)   Praiseworthy Conduct – Reward for Good Works

2:195, 207;
3:134, 148;
4:40, 134;
5:12;
6:160;
10:30;
13:22;

18:46;
22:77, 78;
31:19;
41:34, 35;
42:20, 23, 40;
49:1;
58:11.

(g)   Righteousness and Honour to Parents, Relations and Neighbours:

2:44, 83, 177, 215;
3:92;
4:1, 8, 36;
6:151;
13:21, 25;
16:90;

17:23, 26;
29:8;
30:38;
31:14, 15;
45:15;
107:7

(h)   Uprightness and Asceticism:

1:5, 6;	**42:**15;
10:89;	**46:**13;
11:112;	**72:**16;
16:30;	**81:**28.
41:6, 30;	

(i)   Honour to Orphans, Poor and Travellers:

2:83, 177, 215;	**30:**38;
4:8, 9;	**89:**17, 19;
17:26;	**93:**9, 10.

(j)   Beware the Taunting (Temptation) of People – Seeking Good:

2:266;	**34:**30;
8:25, 28, 39;	**63:**9;
18:46;	**64:**14, 15;
25:20;	**89:**20.

(k)   Fulfilling Covenants: Pardon and Initiative in Good Works:

2:40, 100, 109, 110, 148, 177;	**17:**34;
3:76, 82, 134;	**23:**8, 61;
4:149;	**24:**22;
5:7, 15;	**31:**32;
6:152;	**42:**40;
7:199;	**43:**89;
9:75, 111;	**57:**21;
13:20;	**64:**14;
16:91;	**70:**32.

(l)   Pursuit of Faithfulness and Peace Between Men:

2:244, 280;	**8:**1, 27;
3:75;	**23:**8;
4:58;	**70:**32.

SECTION 25

(HOLY) FEAR and DREAD

(a)   **– of Committing Sin:**

2:281;

4:31, 111, 112;

5:49, 92;

6:15, 16, 120, 151, 164;

7:28, 33;

10:27;

17:16, 32;

24:19;

27:90;

29:4;

30:41;

42:37;

45:21;

53:32;

60:12;

91:10.

(b)   **– Lying to God and Disbelieving His Signs (verses of Qur'an):**

3:94;

4:50;

5:103;

6:21, 27, 49, 93, 124, 150, 157;

7:28, 37, 40, 177, 182;

8:54;

10:17, 21, 68, 69, 95;

11:18;

16:56, 62, 105, 116;

27:74;

29:68;

34:8, 38;

39:33, 60;

45:7, 8, 11;

55:13, 16, 18, 21, 22, 25, 28, 30, 32, 34, 36, 38, 40, 42, 45, 47, 49, 51, 53, 55, 57, 59, 61, 63, 65, 67, 69, 71, 73, 75,77;

61:7;   **62:**5.

(c)   **– Dread of Hypocrisy and Pride:**

4:36, 38, 172, 173;

7:146;

16:23;

17:37, 38;

18:34, 40, 41;

31:18, 19;

35:10;

40:35, 60;

47:33;

57:23;

68:13, 14.

(d)   **Prohibition of Following Passion and Satan and His Deceits:**

2:145, 168, 169, 268;

3:14, 152, 155, 175;

4:27, 38, 76, 83, 117, 119, 120, 135;

5:77, 91;

6:56, 68, 71, 112, 119, 121, 153;
7:27, 30, 200, 202;
8:48;
12:5;
14:22;
16:63, 98, 100;
17:27, 53, 64;
18:28, 50;
20:16;
22:3, 4, 53;
24:21;
25:29;
30:29;
31:21;
35:5, 6;
38:26;
43:36, 38, 63;
45:23;
47:14, 25.

(e)   Dread of Injustice and Cursing:
2:165, 254, 279;
4:40;
5:2, 29, 51, 72, 107;
6:21, 33, 45, 52, 58, 68, 70, 93, 131, 135;
7:33, 44, 45; 180;
8:25;
9:36, 70, 109;
10:39, 44, 52, 54;
11:18, 19, 113, 117;
14:13, 22, 27, 34, 42;
16:33;
19:72;
21:29;
22:25, 53, 60;
25:27, 37;
26:227;
30:41;
40:18, 52;
42:8, 21, 22, 40, 42;
49:11;
61:7;
62:5;
68:12;
85:10.

(f)   Fear of Love of the World:
3:14;
6:32;
10:25. 58;
11:15;
13:26;
15:3;
17:18;
18:7, 28;
28:60;
29:64;
30:36;
31:33;
35:5;
40:39;
42:36;
57:20;
62:11;
75:20;
87:16, 17;
100:8;
102:1.

(g)   Dread of Corruption and Shedding Blood:
2:11, 27, 84, 205;
3:63;

5:33, 64;
7:56;
9:47, 48;
10:23, 40;
11: 85, 116;

13:25;
28:77, 83;
38:28;
47:22, 23.

SECTION 26

HYPOCRITES, UNBELIEVERS and POLYTHEISTS

(a)   **Condition of Hypocrites and their Fate:**
2:8, 20, 76, 78, 204, 206;
3:167, 168;
4:61, 63, 72, 73, 77, 78, 80, 81, 83, 88, 89, 108, 113, 138, 139, 141, 143, 145;
5:41, 52, 53, 61, 81;
6:24;
8:22, 23, 49;
9:42, 45, 47, 49, 50, 53, 59, 62, 66, 75, 80, 82, 87, 94, 98, 101, 125, 127, ·
24:47, 50, 53, 59, 63;
29:10, 11;
33:12, 20, 24, 60, 61, 73;
47:16, 20, 21, 26, 28, 30, 32;
48:6;
58:8, 14, 19;
59:11,13, 16, 17;
63:1-8.

(b)   **Unbelievers – their State and Fate:**
2:6, 7, 26, 28, 39, 90, 98, 104, 105, 108, 126, 135, 161, 162, 165, 167, 170, 171, 206, 210, 212, 253, 254, 257, 276;
3:4, 10, 12, 13, 30, 32, 56, 80, 97, 116, 117, 176, 178, 196, 197;
4:18, 37, 42, 47, 51, 56, 60, 76, 89, 101, 115, 121 136, 137, 150, 151, 167, 168, 170;
5:5, 10, 17, 36, 58, 73, 86, 102, 104, 115;
6:4, 5, 10, 12, 13, 26, 31, 37, 39, 43, 44, 46, 47, 53, 58, 70, 89, 91, 93, 94, 110, 111, 113, 124, 125, 128, 129, 158, 159;
7:5, 6, 27, 28, 36, 38, 40, 51, 53, 64, 182, 183;
8:22, 23, 31, 32, 34, 36, 38 ,52, 55, 59, 71, 73;
9:3, 17, 40, 69, 74, 97, 98;
10:4, 7, 59, 60, 70, 96, 97, 101, 102;

11:9, 10, 16, 19, 22, 27;
13:5, 14, 18, 25, 31, 35;
14:2, 3, 9, 10, 13, 16, 19, 29, 30, 34, 43 49, 50;
15:11, 15;
16:4, 17, 20, 21, 25, 29, 33, 34, 45, 47, 55, 61, 62, 72, 73, 84, 85, 88, 100, 109;
17:48, 59, 72, 98;   **41:**23, 25;
18:29, 42, 43, 53, 101, 103,   **42:**8, 16, 26, 31, 44 ,47;
    104, 106;   **43:**5;
19:69, 73, 75, 81, 83, 86;   **44:**9;
20:74, 125, 126, 129;   **45:**8, 19, 31;
21:8, 39, 42, 44, 98;   **46:**3, 20, 34;
22:19, 22, 25, 44, 66;   **47:**11, 12;
23:44, 56, 63, 68, 81, 106,   **48:**13;
    107, 112, 115;   **50:**23, 28;
24:39, 55;   **57:**19;
25:17, 19, 23, 26 ,77;   **58:**5;
27:5, 64, 85;   **64:**5, 10;
28:61;   **66:**7, 9;
29:22, 23, 25;   **67:**6, 20;
30:7, 34, 45, 59;   **68:**16;
31:6, 25;   **69:**25, 30, 33, 34;
32:12, 20, 22;   **70:**19, 21;
33:8, 64, 66, 68;   **73:**11, 13;
34:38, 40, 42;   **74:**10;
35:6, 7, 26, 36, 37, 39;   **75:**24, 25, 28, 29;
36:70;   **76:**4;
37:34, 62, 72;   **77:**15, 45, 50;
38:2, 27, 55, 64;   **82:**14, 16;
39:1, 22, 24, 26, 32, 47, 48,   **92:**14, 16;
    56, 58, 60;   **98:**6.
40:18, 84, 85;

(c)   **Polytheists – their State and Fate:**
2:22, 165;
4:39, 48, 116, 117, 171;
5:72, 82;
6:14, 19, 22, 23, 25, 41, 43, 56, 58, 64, 71, 81, 88, 100, 106, 109,
    122, 136, 140, 148, 150, 151, 163;
7:33, 174, 190, 195, 197, 198;   **10:**18, 27, 28, 36, 51, 66, 105,
8:22, 23, 73;   106;
9:3, 6;   **11:**101;

12:106;
13:14, 16, 33, 36;
14:22;
15:96;
16:35, 51, 62, 86, 87;
17:2, 22, 23, 39, 40, 42, 111;
18:4-5, 38, 52, 102, 110;
19:81, 88, 92;
21:9, 21, 22, 24, 26, 29, 98, 99;
22:8, 10, 12, 13, 31, 62, 71, 73, 74;
23:59, 117;
24:55;
25:2, 3, 43, 55, 68;
27:59, 60;
28:49, 51, 62, 66, 68, 69, 74, 75;
29:41, 42, 52, 65, 66;

30:13, 28, 31, 33, 40, 42;
31:13, 15, 30;
33:57, 73;
34:22, 23, 27;
35:13, 14, 40;
36:60, 74, 75;
37:35, 161, 163;
39:3, 8, 44, 66;
40:12, 20, 73, 74;
41:6, 9, 47, 48;
42:6, 9, 21;
43:15, 16, 20, 22, 45, 81;
46:4, 7;
48:6;
51:51;
56:46;
57:14, 15;
67:20.

SECTION 27

ADMONITIONS and PROVERBS

(a)   Admonitions:

11:24, 120, 122;	**25:**63;
13:41;	**30:**56;
14:25, 52;	**31:**33;
15:49, 50;	**33:**35;
16:44, 90, 97, 112, 119;	**39:**9, 54, 57, 73, 75;
17:19, 21, 29, 38, 58, 68;	**40:**37, 40;
18:7, 28, 46, 109;	**41:**33;
21:47;	**42:**37;
22:1, 2, 11, 32, 34, 35, 46, 77;	**43:**68, 73.

(b)   Proverbs:

2:17, 19, 26, 171, 261, 264, 266, 274;	**25:**9, 33, 39;
	29:41, 43;
3:117;	**30:**27, 28, 58;
10:24;	**36:**13, 78;
11:24;	**39:**28, 29, 30;
13:17, 19, 35;	**47:**3, 15;
14:18, 24, 26, 45;	**57:**20;
16:60, 74, 76, 112;	**59:**15, 17, 21;
17:48;	**62:**5;
18:32, 45;	**66:**10, 12;
22:45, 73;	**67:**22.
24:35;	

SECTION 28

MERITS OF SPEECH

(a)   The "Dhikr" and the Incitement to it:

2:152, 203, 239;   26:227;
3:191;   30:17;
7:205;   32:15;
8:45;   33:21, 41, 42;
13:28;   39:23;
18:24;   48:9;
19:76;   56:74;
20:124;   59:24;
24:36, 41;   63:9.

(b)   Praise and Thanksgiving: Speaking about the Goodness of God:

1:2;   31:12, 31;
2:152, 172;   34:1, 12;
3:145;   35:1, 12;
5:6;   37:182;
7:43, 58;   39:75;
8:26;   40:61, 65;
9:112;   45:36;
16:75, 78;   64:1;
22:36;   67:23;
23:78;   93:11.
30:18;

(c)   Disseminating Peace:

4:86;   13:24;
6:54;   24:27; 61;
10:10;   33:44;
11:69;   56:26.

(d)   Prayers for the Prophet and Seeking Refuge in God:

7:200;   41:36;
33:56;   113:1, 5;
37:180;   114:1, 6.

(e)   Command to Charity:

2:263;   9:71, 112;
3:104, 110;   22:41;
4:9;   31:17;
5:79;   40:41, 44.
7:199;

(f)   On Saying "God Willing" etc.:

2:83;   33:70;
17:28, 53;   35:10;
18:22, 23, 39;   27:180, 181, 182.
20:44;

(g)   Command to "Seek Forgiveness" (that is for compliments paid to one):

3:17, 135;   41:6;
4:64, 106, 110;   71:10, 12;
5:33;   73:20.
11:3;

(h)   Calling on God: His Answer to "Believers":

1:5, 7;   25:65, 74;
2:126, 129, 186, 201, 202,   27:19, 40, 62;
    286;   30:33;
3:8, 9, 16, 38, 147, 192, 194; 31:32;
4:32, 75;   32:16;
6:43, 63, 64;   40:60;
7:29, 47, 55, 56, 156, 180,   41:49;
    205;   42:26;
10:10, 12, 22;   46:15;
14:34, 41;   59:10;
17:65, 67, 110;   60:4, 5;
21:87, 89;   66:8.
23:118;

SECTION 29

EVIL SPEAKING

2:142, 225;
4:112, 148;
6:24, 93;
17:11, 36;
18:54, 56;
22:30;
23:3;

24:11·
25:72;
26:224, 227;
49:12;
68:11;
104:1.

SECTION 30

BEGINNING OF CREATION

(a)   **Creation of the Throne, "Tablet" and Pen:**

2:255;	**22**:70;
7:54;	**32**:4;
10:3;	**35**:11;
11:7;	**36**:12;
13:2, 39;	**50**:4;
17:58;	**68**:1;
20:5;	**69**:17.

(b)   **Creation of Angels:**

2:30, 32, 34, 255;	**42**:5;
3:39, 124;	**43**:16, 17, 19;
4:172;	**50**:17, 18;
6:61, 93;	**51**:4;
7:206;	**53**:27, 28;
13:11;	**58**:4;
16:49, 50;	**68**:1;
21:19, 22, 26, 28;	**70**:3, 4;
22:75;	**74**:31;
25:25, 59;	**77**:1, 4, 5;
35:1;	**81**:20, 21, 23;
37:164, 166;	**82**:10, 12;
39:76;	**86**:4.
40:7, 15;	

(c)   **Creation of the World:**

2:29;	**43**:12;
6:101, 102;	**51**:49;
25:2;	**54**:49, 50;
30:19;	**57**:1;
32:7;	**61**:1;
36:36;	**62**:1;
39:63;	**64**:1;
40:62;	**81**:15, 18;
42:49;	**86**:1-3;

91:1-8;   95:1-3.
92:3;

(d)   Creation of Seven Heavens:
2:22, 29, 164;   38:27;
3:190;   39:6, 39, 47;
6:73, 101;   40:57, 64;
7:54;   41:9, 12;
9:36;   42:29;
10:3, 6;   43:10;
11:7;   44:38, 39;
13:2, 4;   45:3, 28;
14:19, 32;   46:3, 33;
15:16, 20, 85;·   50:6-7, 38;
16:3;   51:7, 47, 48;
18:51;   52:5;
20:4, 53;   55:7, 10;
21:16, 32, 81;   57:4;
25:59 ,61;   64:3;
27:60, 61;   65:12;
29:44, 61;   67:3, 5, 15;
30:8, 22, 25;   77:9, 25, 27;
32:4;   78:6, 12;
34:1;   79:27, 31;
35:1;   85:1;
37:5, 10;   86:11, 12.

(e)   Creation of Water, Seas and Rivers:
2:84;   25:49, 53;
6:6;   27:61;
11:7;   31:32;
13:3;   35:12;
16:14, 15;   36:34;
21:30;   52:6;
24:39, 40;   55:19, 20.

(f)   Creation of Mountains and Plains :
13:3;   23:20;
15:19;   27:61, 88;
16:15; 81;   31:32;
21:31;   35:27;

41:10;
50:7;
52:1, 10;

77:27;
78:6;
79:32.

(g)   Creation of Sun, Moon and Stars:
7:54;
10:5;
13:2;
14:33;
16:12,
21:33;
25:61;
29:61;
31:29;
35:13;

36:38, 40;
37:5, 6;
39:6;
41:37;
55:5, 17;
74:32;
77:8;
78:13;
81:1, 2.

(h)   Creation of Night and Day:
2:164;
3:27, 190;
6:1, 96;
7:54;
10:6, 67;
13:3;
14:33;
16:12;
17:12;
21:33, 87;
22:47, 61;
24:35, 40, 44;
25:47, 62;
27:86;

28:73;
31:29;
35:13;
36:37, 40;
39:5;
40:23;
41:37;
45:5;
74:33, 34;
81:17, 18;
83:17;
89:1-4;
92:1, 2.

(i)   Creation of Clouds, Lightning and Thunder:
2:19, 22, 164, 265;
6:6, 99;
7:57;
8:11;
10:22, 24;
13:12, 13, 17;
15:22;
16:10, 65;
17:69;

20:53;
21:30;
22:23;
23:18;
24:43;
25:45, 48;
27:60, 63;
29:63;
30:19, 24, 46, 48, 49, 51;

32:27;
34:2;
35:2, 9, 27;
39:22;
40:13;
41:39;
42:28, 33;

43:11;
45:5;
50:9;
51:1, 2;
77:1, 3;
78:14;
80:25, 26.

(j)   Creation of Plants and Trees:

2:22, 164;
6:99;
10:24;
13:3, 4;
14:32;
15:19;
16:10, 11, 13, 67;
18:45;
20:53, 54;
22:5, 63;
23:19, 20;
24:35;
25:10, 49;
27:60;

30:19, 24, 50, 51;
32:27;
34:2;
35:9, 27;
36:23, 34, 80;
39:21;
41:39;
50:7, 9, 11;
55:6, 11, 12;
57:20;
78:15, 16;
80:27, 32;
87:4, 5.

(k)   Creation of Soul and Spirit:

6:6, 98, 122;
7:172;
17:85;
30:28;

31:28;
32:9;
39:7.

(l)   Creation of Djinn:

6:100, 128;
7:27;
15:18, 28;
26:221, 223;

27:39;
34:12, 14;
55:15;
72:1, 25.

(m)   Creation of Adam and Eve: expulsion from Heaven (and the Devil's attitude to them):

2:30, 31, 33, 37;
3:33, 59;
4:1, 118, 120;
6:2;

7:12, 23, 189;
15:26, 28, 43;
17:61, 64;
18:50;

20:115, 123;
23:12;
30:21;
32:7;

38:71, 85;
39:7;
55:3, 4, 14;
76:1.

(n)   Creation of Man – Forming Him in the Womb:

2:21;
3:6;
7:11, 189;
16:4, 70, 78;
17:11;
18:37, 51;
20:55;
21:37, 104;
22:5;
23:13, 14, 78;
24:45;
25:49, 54;
27:64;
29:19, 20;
30:11, 20, 23, 27, 40, 45;
32:8;
35:11, 28;
36:77, 79, 81;
37:11;

39:7;
40:64, 67, 98;
42:11;
45:4;
46:15;
49:13;
50:15, 16;
53:32, 45, 47;
64:2-3;
67:23, 24;
75:37, 39;
76:2;
78:8;
82:7, 8;
85:13;
86:5-7, 10;
90:4;
95:4, 5;
96:2.

(o)   Creation of Reason – Man's Highest Attribute:

2:170, 171, 242;
23:80;
24:61;
28:60;
29:35, 43, 63;
30:24, 28;
34:46;
36:62, 68;

37:138;
40:67;
43:3;
45:5;
49:4;
52:17;
59:14.

(p)   Creation of Cattle and Wild Animals:

5:2;
16:5, 8;
22:30;
23:21, 22;
24:45;

25:49;
26:133;
35:28;
36:42, 71, 73;
39:6;

40:79, 80;   **45:**4;
42:11, 29;   **100:**1, 5.
43:12, 13;

(q)   Duty of Pondering Creation:
2:26;   **21:**30;
3:191;   **26:**7;
6:95, 104;   **27:**14;
7:185;   **30:**8;
10:3, 101;   **37:**73;
12:105;   **39:**42;
13:3;   **50:**8;
16:48, 66, 79;   **67:**2-3;
18:8;   **88:**17, 20.
20:128;

.

SECTION 31

STORIES OF THE PROPHETS

(a)   **Mission of Prophets and Sending Down on them of the (Holy) Books:**

2:136, 213;

3:84, 146;

4:163;

6:48, 86;

7:35, 43, 53;

10:74;

12:110, 111;

13:38;

14:4, 9, 15, 47;

15:10;

16:2, 35, 36, 43, 44, 84, 89;

17:56;

19:58;

20:18;

21:7, 25;

22:52, 75;

23:44, 51;

25:20, 51;

28:59, 75;

30:47;

33:7;

34:34, 45;

35:24, 25;

37:171, 173, 181;

38:14;

40:5, 22, 50, 51, 78, 83;

42:2, 13, 51;

43:6, 7;

57:25;

58:21;

64:6;

72:27, 28;

77:1.

(b)   **Adam and Eve Sent Down to Earth:**

2:38;

7:24, 26.

(c)   **Noah and His People:**

2:33, 34;

4:163;

6:84;

7:59, 64, 69;

9:70;

10:71, 73;

11:25, 48;

14:9;

17:3, 17;

21:76, 77;

22:42;

23:23, 30;

25:37;

26:105, 121;

29:14, 15;

33:7;

37:75, 82;

38:12;

40:5;

51:46;

54:9, 16;

57:26;

69:11, 12;   **71:**1, 28.

(d)   Abraham:
2:124, 125, 127, 133, 135, 136, 140, 258, 260;
3:33, 34, 65, 67, 68, 84, 90;   **22:**26, 27, 43, 78;
4:54, 125, 163;   **26:**69, 89;
6:74, 80, 83, 84, 161;   **29:**16, 19, 24, 31;
9:70, 114;   **33:**7;
11:69, 76;   **37:**83, 113;
12:6;   **38:**45, 47;
14:35, 41;   **43:**26, 28;
15:51, 58;   **51:**24, 37;
16:120, 123;   **57:**26;
19:41, 50;   **60:**4.
21:51, 73;

(e)   Isaac:
2:123, 136, 140;   **6:**84;
3:84;   **12:**6;
4:163;   **14:**39

(f)   Jacob:
2:132, 133, 136, 140;   **6:**84;
3:84;   **12:**6, 68.
4:163;

(g)   Ishmael:
2:127, 133, 136, 140;   **14:**39;
3:84;   **19:**54, 55;
4:163;   **21:**85, 86;
6:86;   **38:**48.

(h)   Idriss:
19:56, 57;   **21:**85.

(i)   Elias:
6:86;   **38:**48.

(j)   Jonah:
4:163;   **10:**98;
6:86;   **21:**87, 88;

37:139, 148

(k)   Lot and his People:

6:86;	**26:**160, 174;
7:80, 84;	**27:**54, 59;
11:77, 83;	**29:**28, 35;
15:59, 79;	**37:**133, 138;
21:71, 74, 75;	**38:**13;
22:43;	**54:**33, 39;
25:40;	**69:**9, 10.

(l)   Hud and his People:

7:65, 72;	**41:**15, 16;
11:50, 60;	**46:**21, 28;
23:31, 41;	**51:**41, 42;
26:123, 139;	**54:**18, 21;
38:12;	**69:**6-8.

(m)   Salih and his People:

7:73, 79;	**38:**13;
11:61, 68;	**54:**23, 31;
17:59;	**69:**5;
26:141, 158;	**91:**11, 15.
27:45, 53;	

(n)   David:

2:247, 251;	**21:**78, 79;
4:163;	**27:**15;
5:78;	**34:**10, 11;
6:84;	**38:**17, 26, 30.
17:55;	

(o)   Solomon:

2:102;	**27:**15, 25, 27, 44;
4:163;	**34:**12, 14;
6:84;	**38:**30, 40.
21:78, 79, 81, 82;	

(p)   Job:

4:163	**21:**83, 84;
6:84;	**38:**41, 44

(q)   Joseph:
6:84;   12:4, 56, 58, 101.

(r)   Moses:
2:49, 55, 65, 73, 87, 92, 136;
3:11, 84;
4:153, 163, 164;
5:20, 24, 26;
6:84, 91,154;
7:103, 104, 106, 146, 148, 155, 159, 171;
8:52, 54;   28:3, 49, 52, 55;
10:75, 93;   32:23, 24;
11:17, 96, 99, 110;   33:7, 69;
14:5-8;   37:114, 122;
17:2, 101, 104;   40:23, 46, 53, 54;
18:60, 82;   41:45;
19:51, 53;   43:46, 56;
20:9, 14, 17, 52, 56, 97;   44:17, 33;
21:84;   45:16, 17;
22:44;   51:38, 40;
23:42, 45, 48;   54:41, 42;
25:35, 36;   61:5;
26:10, 67;   69:9.
27:7, 14;

(s)   Shiab (Jethro)
7:85, 93;   29:36, 37.
11:84, 95;

(t)   Zechariah:
3:37, 41;   19:2, 15;
6:85;   21:89, 90.
(u)   Jesus and his Mother Mary:
2:87, 136, 253;   21:91;
3:33, 37, 42, 43, 45, 55, 59,   23:50;
   84;   33:7;
4:156, 158, 163, 171, 172;   34:57, 59, 61, 63, 65;
5:17, 46, 72, 75, 78, 110, 118;   57:27;
6:85;   61:6, 14.
19:16, 34, 36, 39;

(v)   Elijah:

6:85;   **37:**123, 132.

SECTION 32

HISTORICAL NARRATIVES

(a)   **Cain and Abel:**
5:27, 31.

(b)   **'Ad and Thamud:**

9:70;	**29:**38;
10:80, 84;	**41:**17, 18;
14:9;	**51:**43, 45;
22:42, 44;	**89:**6, 9.
25:38;	

(c)   **Story of One Slain and Raised by God:**
2:259ff.

(d)   **Story of Moses and Pharoah:**

28:76, 82;	**29:**39, 40.

(e)   **Story of Fellows of the Cave:**
18:9, 22, 25, 26.

(f)   **Luqman :**
31:12, 13, 16, 19.

(g)   **Balaam:**
7:175, 177.

(h)   **Alexander the Great:**
18:83, 98.

(i)   **Days of Ignorance:**

5:103;	**9:**30;
6:142, 144;	**16:**58, 59.
8:35;	

(j)   **Stories of Cities and People that have Perished:**

2:134, 141;	**3:**137;

6:6, 38, 42;
7:4, 34, 38, 93, 102;
9:70, 120;
10:13, 19, 47 ,49, 98;
11:102, 103, 116, 117;
12:111;
14:9;
15:4, 5;
16:112;
17:58;
18:59, 74, 98;
20:128;
21:6, 11, 15, 95;

22:45, 48, 67;
23:43, 53;
25:38;
26:208;
28:45, 58, 59;
30:2, 6;
32:26;
33:13;
34:18;
35:11;
38:3;
47:13;
79:26.

SECTION 33

PEOPLE OF THE BOOK

(a)   The Children of Israel:
1:7;
2:40, 97, 102, 103, 111, 113, 118, 120, 122, 123, 135, 140, 211, 246, 247;
3:21, 24, 71, 93, 112, 181, 184;
4:44, 66, 68, 137, 153, 157, 160, 161;
5:12, 13, 21, 24, 26, 32, 43, 60, 62, 64, 70, 71, 78, 81, 110;

6:91, 146;	**58:**8;
9:10, 30, 31;	**59:**2, 5;
16:118, 124;	**60:**13;
17:4, 8;	**62:**6, 8.
57:37;	

(b)   Christians – Pastors and Priests:

1:7;	**9:**30, 31, 34;
2:62, 113, 120, 135, 140;	**57:**27, 29.
5:14, 73, 77, 82, 85;	

(c)   Corruption of the Heavenly Book:

4:46;	**5:**13, 41.

(d)   Dispute Between Jews and Christians:

2:113, 140;	**42:**14.
5:18, 64;	

(e)   Bitter Enmity of Jews to Believers:

5:82;	**59:**14.

(f)   Prohibition of Disputing with People of Book:

29:46;	**42:**16.

(g)   Information about Peoples of the Book:
2:109, 111, 118, 121, 145, 146;
3:19, 20, 64, 65, 70, 72, 73, 75, 78, 79, 98, 100, 110, 113, 115, 117, 120, 187, 188, 199;

4:44, 46, 47 ,51, 55, 123, 153, 159, 171;
5:15, 41 ,42, 57, 59, 65, 66, 68, 77;
13:36;
34:6.

SECTION 34

MUHAMMAD
(on him be prayers and peace)

(a)   **Message of Abraham, Moses and Jesus Concerning Him:**

2:89, 129;   61:6.

7:157;

(b)   **His General Message, Mission: a Mercy to the Worlds:**

2:101, 119, 151, 252;   35:24;

3:68, 144, 164;   36:2-5;

4:79, 166, 170, 174;   37:37;

6:19, 50;   39:12, 33;

7:158;   40:66;

8:33;   41:33;

9:33, 128;   42:52, 53;

13:30, 43;   43:43;

16:113;   44:18;

17:96, 105;   45:18;

21:107;   47:14;

22:67;   48:8, 28, 29;

23:73;   53:2-3;

27:79;   61:9;

29:52;   62:2;

33:40, 45;   64:12;

34:28;   98:2.

(c)   **"Descent" of Inspiration on him (first and last verses of Qur'an):**

2:53, 99, 285;   15:49, 50, 87, 94;

3:58, 60;   16:2, 64, 82, 89, 123;

4:113, 163;   17:39, 41, 42, 86, 94, 95, 106;

5:67;   18:1, 27, 28, 110;

6:19, 50, 106, 145;   19:97;

10:2, 15, 71, 104, 106, 109;   20:2-4, 99, 114;

11:49, 112, 115;   21:3, 10, 45, 50, 108;

12:2, 108;   22:16, 67;

13:1, 30, 36, 40;   24:1, 34, 54;

78

25:1;
26:193, 194;
27:6, 91, 92;
28:87;
29:45, 47;
32:2;
33:2, 39, 46;
34:50;
35:24, 31;
36:69;
38:4, 70;
39:42, 65;
40:15;
41:6, 44;
42:3, 7, 13, 15, 48, 52;
43:43, 44;
44:58;

45:6;
46:9, 29, 32;
47:2;
50:2;
51:55;
53:2-7, 10;
55:2;
57:9;
62:2;
65:11;
74:2;
75:16, 19;
76:23;
87:6, 7;
88:21;
96:1, 3.

(d)   His "Glad Tidings" and Warnings:

2:119;
5:19;
6:19, 51;
7:184, 188;
10:2;
11:2, 12;
13:7;
14:44;
15:89;
16:2;
17:105;
18:2, 4;
19:97;
25:1, 56;
26:194;
28:46;
29:50;

32:3;
33:45;
34:28, 44, 46;
35:23, 24;
36:6, 70;
38:65, 70;
39:17, 18;
40:15, 18;
42:7;
46:9, 12;
48:8;
51:50, 51;
53:56;
67:17, 26;
74:2;
87:9, 10.

(e)   Mention of Muhammad in Books of Prophets:

2:100, 101, 146;
3:81;
5:16, 19;

6:20, 114;
7:157;
13:43;

26:196;
28:52, 54;
29:47;
33:7;
46:10;

47:32;
48:29;
57:28;
98:4.

(f)   Belief in Muhammad and Obedience to Him:
3:31, 32, 132, 153;
4:13, 59, 69, 80, 115;
5:92;
7:158;
8:20, 24, 46;
9:61, 71;
11:5, 8;
24:52, 56;
25:41;

26:6, 216;
33:31, 33, 36, 53, 57, 71;
35:4;
37:12;
47:33;
48:17;
57:7;
61:11;
64:8, 12.

(g)   God's Reproof of Muhammad as Friend to Friend:
3:128, 159;
6:52;
9:43, 80;
10:94;
11:12, 17;

17:75;
33:37;
66:1;
79:43, 45;
80:1, 11.

(h)   His Teaching and Guidance to His People:
2:136, 151;
3:164;
6:90, 126, 161;
7:157, 203;
11:114;
12:104;
13:36;
14:1;

18:27, 110;
23:72;
25:57;
38:86;
42:15, 23;
43:47;
52:40;
81:24.

(i)   The Djinn Believe in Him
72:1, 15;

(j)   His Victories and Assistance of Angels and Djinn
2:214;
3:124, 125;
5:11, 67;

8:9, 62;
9:40;
11:120;

15:95;
17:74;
22:15;
25:22;
33:9;

39:37;
44:59;
47:27;
48:3-4, 23, 24, 26.

(k)   His Pilgrimage:
9:40, 117;
43:41, 42;

74:5.

(l)   Prophet's Share of Spoils:
8:41;

44:59.

(m)   "Battle" of Badr:
3:123;
8:17, 19, 25, 41, 43, 44, 48, 50, 68.

(n)   "Battle" of Uhud:
3:121, 122.

(o)   "Battle" of The Trench:
33:20, 22, 25, 27.

(p)   "Battle" of Hudabiyya:
9:1-2.

48:1, 22, 24.

(q)   "Battle" of Hunein:
9:25, 27.

(r)   "Battle" of Qureiza:
8:27, 56, 58;
9:101;

48:2;
59:5, 6.

(s)   "Battle" of Kheibar:
59:11, 15;

(t)   "Battle" of Tabuk:
9:40, 65, 101.

(u)   Conquest of Mecca, Tait and Bishara:

5:3;   28:85;
6:92;   32:29, 30;
8:43, 64;   48:2, 27;
9:40;   110:1-3.
17:60;

(v)   Muhammad's Concern for the Guidance of His People:

4:64;   26:3, 215;
9:128;   33:6, 45;
15:88;   48:19.
16:125;

(w)   His Opposition to "Unbelievers":

2:120, 145;   40:66;
9:84, 85, 113, 129;   42:15;
13:37;   45:18, 19;
15:94;   51:54;
25:52;   53:29;
26:239;   54:6;
27:80;   68:8, 16;
28:56, 86;   70:42;
33:1, 39, 48;   76:24;
37:174, 175;   88:22.
39:65;

(x)   His Exalted Position and God's Favour to Him:

3:44;   47:19;
4:79, 113;   48:2 ,8;
9:117;   53:5, 10, 11, 17, 18;
12:101, 103;   58:12, 13;
15:87;   66:8;
17:79, 87;   68:2-4;
25:10;   87:8;
26:219;   93:1, 11;
28:44, 46;   94:1-8;
29:48;   96:5;
33:56;   108:1.

(y)   The Names Given Him by God in the Qur'an:

3:144;   20:1;
9:128;   23:40;

36:1;   **73:**1;
47:2;   **74:**1;
48:29;   **88:**21.
61:6;

(z)   God Swears by Muhammad and His City, Mecca:
20:1;   **90:**1, 3;
36:1;   **103:**1.

(aa)   God Commands Prayer and Praise for His Prophet:
9:108;   **56:**74, 96;
15:98, 99;   **73:**1-8, 20;
30:130, 132;   **74:**3;
28:93;   **76:**25, 26;
29:45;   **87:**1;
39:10, 12, 13, 15, 67;   **96:**19;
40:55, 56;   **108:**2;
50:39, 40;   **110:**3.
52:48, 49;

(bb)   Muhammad's Wives (and the matter of Zeinab):
33:2, 28, 33, 37 ,50, 53, 59;   **66:**3, 5.

(cc)   God's Grace to Him in Forgiving His Sins:
7:199;   **68:**4;
48:2;   **74:**6.

(dd)   God Solaces His Prophet:
2:272;   **20:**130;
5:41;   **21:**41;
6:33; 35, 107, 112, 116, 135,   **22:**42, 53, 67;
   147, 159;   **23:**54, 56;
7:2;   **24:**57;
8:5;   **25:**20, 31, 33;
10:41, 42, 46, 65;   **26:**3;
12:103;   **27:**70, 80, 81;
13:31, 32;   **28:**56;
15:3, 10, 97;   **30:**52;
16:63, 82, 103, 127;   **31:**23;
17:77;   **33:**60;
18:6;   **35:**4, 8, 25;
19:84;   **36:**76;

37:149;
38:12;
40:4;
41:13, 43;
42:6, 48;
43:22, 23, 40, 83, 89;
47:13;
50:36;
51:52;

52:29, 30, 45;
68:44, 45;
70:42;
73:10, 12;
79:15;
85:17, 18.

(ee)   His People, Their Honour, Relief of their Distress:
2:143, 185;
3:110;
5:6;
7:181;
8:68;
10:14;
21:10;

22:78;
23:52, 53;
24:61;
33:5, 38, 50
45:14;
73:20.

(ff)   The Virtues of His "Companions" (Ashab):
2:108, 214;
3:159;
9:100;
11:17;
24:63;
33:23, 24;
39:34, 35;
47:20;

48:4-9, 29;
49:1-5, 7-8;
57:10;
59:10;
62:2-3;
66:5;
92:5-7;
103:3.

(gg)   His Helpers (Ansar) and Household:
8:72, 74;
9:40, 117;
11:73;
28:61;

33:33, 34;
42:23, 38;
59:9.

(hh)   His General Intercession:
17:79, 80;
23:97, 98;

28:88.

(ii)   Denial of (His) Insanity and Magic:
10:2;

34:46;

38:4;   81:22.
51:52;

(jj)   God's Command to Him of Patience:
21:112;   50:39;
23:96;   52:48;
30:60;   68:48;
33:3, 48;   70:5;
38:17;   73:9, 10;
40:55, 77;   74:7;
46:35;   76:24.

.

**(kk)   Superiority of His Religion Over all Other Religions & the
         Cancelling of all Other by His Law:**
3:85;   48:28;
5:3;   61 :8-9;
9:33, 48;   98:1-3.
15:9;
21:44;

**(ll)   What God Related to His Prophet About Previous Prophets &
         Peoples:**
2:258, 259;   54:9, 18, 23, 33, 41;
11:49, 100, 120;   57:26, 27;
12:3, 109, 111;   60:4;
15:51;   61:5-6;
18:83;   64:5;
19:98;   65:8,10;
20:99;   66:10, 12;
25:40;   68:48, 50;
28:3;   79:15, 26;
40:78;   85:4, 10, 17, 18;
43:45;   87 :18, 19;
46:12;   89:6, 7, 9, 14;
51:24, 38 ,41, 43, 46;   105:1-5.

**(mm)   Information About What the Prophet Endured From the
         Qureish in Preaching to Them:**
2:23, 118, 170;   10:15, 16, 49, 51, 53, 57, 59,
8:42, 47;   104, 108;
9:13, 74;   11:5, 8, 14;
                                     13:5-6, 30, 42;

14:28;
15:3, 85 ,90, 97;
16:1, 43 ,45, 83, 101, 125;
17:46, 56, 57, 76;
18:55, 57, 58;
19:77, 80;
20:133, 135;
21:36, 41, 46, 109, 111;
22:19, 25, 47, 49, 68, 69;
23:56, 69, 71, 75, 77, 93, 95;
25:7-9, 27, 29, 40, 44, 52;
26:4-8, 192, 197, 208, 212, 214;
27:72;
28:47;
29:51, 53 ,54, 67;
30:6, 10, 28;
31:7, 21 ,24;
32:3, 28, 30;
34:3, 28, 33, 43, 44, 46 ,51, 54;
35:3, 5, 37, 42, 43;
36:6, 11;
37:11, 13, 34, 50, 61, 149, 158, 167, 170, 176 ,179;
38:2, 11, 15, 16;
39:36, 39 ,40, 49, 52;
40:6, 10, 12, 56, 69, 77;
41:5-6, 13, 14, 26, 29, 33, 38, 40, 42, 54;
42:13, 15, 24, 47;
43:9, 29, 32, 57, 59, 79, 80, 88;
44:10, 16, 34, 37;
45:6-9, 10, 21, 25, 26, 35;
46:7, 11, 35;
47:1-3, 8, 10, 14, 22;
48:25, 26;
50:3, 5-6, 12, 14, 22, 36, 37, 45;

51:8, 14, 53, 54, 59, 60;
52:15, 16;
53:19, 26, 33, 37, 59 ,61;
54:2-5, 43, 45, 47, 48, 51;
56:81, 87;
57:8;
58:20;
60:1-2;
61:8;
64:10;
67:9, 11, 13, 18, 25, 30;
68:5-6, 9, 17, 35, 43, 46, 47, 51;
69:38, 43, 44, 47, 49, 50;
70:1-3, 6, 15, 36, 39;
73:15, 19;
74:11, 30, 49, 54, 56;
75:20, 21, 31, 35;
76:27,28;
77:7, 16 ,22, 24, 28;
78:1, 17, 40;
79:27, 33, 37, 39, 43, 44, 46;
80:17, 23;
81:26;
83:13, 16, 29, 33;
84:20, 24;
85:10, 19, 20;
86:17;
87:10, 13;
88:23, 24;
89:15, 20;
90:19, 20;
92:8, 11;
96:6, 19;
102:1-8;
103:2;
106:1-4;
107:1-3;
111:1-5.

(ii)   The Arguments of the Infidels with Him:

2:139;	**25:**4, 21, 22, 32;
3:61;	**27:**70, 71;
6:7, 10, 91, 135, 164;	**28:**57;
7:3;	**29:**12, 13, 50, 61, 63;
8:30;	**32:**28;
9:32, 61;	**34:**24, 27, 50;
10:2, 38, 49;	**36:**69, 70;
11:7, 12;	**37:**36, 38, 40;
13:7, 16, 27, 31, 43;	**39:**64;
14:46;	**41:**43;
15:6-7, 90, 91;	**43:**24, 25;
16:44, 101, 102;	**52:**30, 47;
17:50, 51, 73, 90, 93;	**53:**30;
20:133;	**86:**15, 16;
21:3-5, 34;	**108:**3;
22:15;	**109:**1-6.

(jj)   The Farewell Pilgrimage:
5:3.

(kk)   God's Announcement of His (Muhammad's) Death:

3:144;	**39:**31;
21:34;	**110:**1-3.

SECTION 35

SEDITION, DISCORD and THE LAST DAY (The Hour)

(a)   **Descent of Jesus and Going Forth of Gog and Magog:**

4:159;   **27:**82;

18:94, 98;   **43:**61.

21:96;

(b)   **Infidels Refuse to Believe on Announcement of Last Day:**

6:158;   **23:**99, 100;

15:2;   **44:**12.

16:28;

(c)   **Smoke of Splitting of Mountains:**

20:105, 106;   **73:**14;

44:10, 11;   **77:**10;

56:5-6;   **78:**20;

69:14;   **81:**3.

(d)   **Sudden Occurrence of "The Hour":**

6:31, 134;   **42:**17, 18;

7:187;   **43:**66, 85;

12:107;   **45:**27, 32;

15:85;   **47:**18;

16:77;   **52:**9, 10;

17:51;   **53:**42, 57, 58;

18:47;   **54:**1-6, 46;

20:15;   **55:**33, 37, 39;

21:1, 40, 49, 97, 104;   **56:**1-7;

22:1-2, 7, 55;   **69:**15, 16;

30:12, 14, 43, 55, 57;   **79:**6, 12;

31:34;   **81:**1-8, 11;

33:63;   **84:**1-5;

34:3;   **88:**1-7;

35:41;   **89:**21, 23;

40:59;   **99:**1-6;

41:47;   **101:**1-5.

SECTION 36

THE (DAY OF) RESURRECTON

(a)   No Soul Will Die Until its Time Comes:
7:34;   16:70.
13:38;

(b)   Death and Mortal Throes:

2:28;   30:40;
3:145, 185;   32:11;
4:78;   39:31, 43;
5:106;   40:68;
6:60, 61, 93;   41:30;
7:34;   44:8, 29;
9:116;   50:19;
11:7;   53:44;
16:32, 61, 70;   55:26, 27;
21:35;   63:10, 11;
22:5, 66;   67:2;
23:15;   75:26;
28:88;   102:2.
29:57;

(c)   Infidelity of Those Who Deny Resurrection:

13:5;   34:7-8, 21;
16:38, 60;   36:78, 79;
17:10, 49, 51, 98;   38:26;
18:48;   39:45;
19:66, 67;   41:7, 50;
20:102, 104;   42:18;
21:38;   44:34, 36;
22:5;   45:24, 32, 34;
23:74, 82, 83;   46:17, 18;
25:11, 21;   53:27;
27:4, 66;   64:7;
29:23;   82:9;
30:8, 55;   83:10, 12.
32:10, 12, 14;

(d)   The Trumpet Blasts:

6:73;
18:99;
20:102, 106;
23:101;
27:87;
36:51;
37:16, 33;
39:69;

50:20, 41, 42;
52:45;
69:13;
74:8;
78:18, 19;
79:34, 35;
80:33, 42.

(e)   Resurrection (and Gathering Together):

2:28, 203, 245;
3:185;
4:69, 87;
5:109;
6:12, 22, 36, 38, 60, 72, 94,
     128, 130, 164;
7:29;
8:24;
10:4, 20, 23, 28, 45;
11:4-7, 103, 108;
14:21, 48;
15:25;
16:38, 39, 111;
17:52, 71, 97;
18:44, 47, 48;
19:40, 68, 85;
20:102, 111;
22:7, 66;
23:15, 16, 100;
24:64;
25:17;
27:65, 83;
29:19, 57;
30:11, 25, 40, 56;
32:11;

34:40;
35:18;
36:12, 32, 51, 83;
39:45;
40:15, 77, 78;
42:47;
43:14, 85;
45:26;
46:6; 33;
50:20, 42, 44;
54:7-8;
58:6, 9;
64:3;
67:24; ·
69:1-3;
70:42, 44;
75:1-4, 7, 12, 30, 39;
78:39;
79:13, 14;
82:1-4;
83:5;
85:2;
88:8-9, 11, 16, 25;
100:9.

(f)   The Balance and the Books

7:8-9;

17:13, 14, 71;

18:49;
21:47;
23:102, 103;
39:70;
40:17;
45:29, 33;
54:52, 53;
55:7;

58:6;
69:19, 21, 25;
78:29;
81:10;
83:7;
84:7; 10;
101:6-9.

(g) **The Accounting (Judgment) and Separation of Peoples:**

2:202;
10:54;
21:35;
22:17;
23:62;
24:25, 38, 39;
27:78;
28:74;
29:13;
31:33;
32:25;
39:32, 47, 60, 69;
40:16, 20, 48, 51, 78;
43:34, 39;
44:40, 42;
45:28;
50:21;

51:6;
55:31, 41;
56:7, 12;
62:8;
64:9;
69:18;
75:13;
76:11, 13;
77:35, 40;
78:17, 38;
81:8-9, 14;
82:5-6, 15, 19;
83:34, 36;
84:8-9;
88:26;
89:24, 26.

(h) **Testimony Against Worshippers:**

24:24;
36:65;
41:20, 21;

75:14, 15;
100:7.

(i) **Intercession:**

2:123, 255;
19:87;
20:109;

43:86;
78:38.

(j) **Paradise and What God Has Prepared for Those Who Get There:**

2:25, 82, 214, 221;
3:15, 133, 136, 185, 195, 198;

4:13, 57, 122, 124;
5:12, 72, 119;

7:40, 42, 44, 46, 47;
9:21, 22, 72, 89, 100;
10:9, 10, 26;
11:23, 108;
13:23, 24, 35;
14:23;
15:45, 48;
16:31, 32;
18:31, 107, 108;
19:60, 63;
20:76;
21:102, 103;
22:14, 23;
23:11;
25:16, 75, 76;
26:90;
28:61;
29:58;
31:8-9;
32:19;
34:1;
35:33, 35;
36:55, 58;
37:41, 49, 61;
38:50, 54;
39:21, 74, 75;
40:40;
43:7, 73;
44:52, 57;
46:14;
47:6, 12, 15;
48:5;
50:31, 34, 35;
51:15;
52:17, 20, 22, 28;
55:46, 48, 50, 52, 54, 56, 58, 62, 64, 66, 68, 70, 72, 74, 76;
56:15, 23, 25, 26, 40, 88, 91, 95;
57:10, 12;
58:22;
64:9;
65:11;
66:8;
68:34;
69:22, 24;
70:35;
74:39, 40;
76:5-6, 12, 22;
77:41, 44;
78:32, 35;
81:13;
85:11;
88:10, 16;
98:8.

(k)   The Fire (Hell) and What God Has Prepared – Torment:
2:24, 80, 81, 126, 167, 206;
3:10, 131, 115;
4:14, 56, 169;
5:10, 72;
6:27, 70, 128;
7:38, 41, 50, 179;
8:37;
9:17, 35, 63, 68, 73, 109;
10:4-8;
11:106, 107, 119;
13:5, 18;
15:43, 44;
17:8, 18, 97;
18:29, 100;
19:86;
21:98, 100;
22:19, 22, 51, 72;
23:104, 107, 108, 112, 114;
25:11, 14, 34, 65, 66;
26:91, 103;
29:54, 55, 68;
32:13, 14, 20, 21;

33:64, 65;
35:36, 37;
36:59, 67;
37:161, 163;
38:55, 61;
39:15, 17, 61, 72;
40:6, 46 ,60, 71, 72, 76;
41:19;
42:45;
43:74, 75, 77;
44:43, 50;
47:15;
50:23, 29, 30;
52:13, 14, 16;
55:35, 43, 44;
56:41, 56, 92, 95;

57:15, 19;
58:8;
59:17;
66:6;
67:6, 11;
69:31, 32, 35, 37;
70:15, 18;
74:26, 31, 35, 37, 48;
77:29, 34;
78:21, 28, 30;
79:39;
81:12;
98:6;
101:10, 11;
104:4,9.

(l)   Separation between Heaven and Hell etc. :

2:46;
7:44; 46;
10:26;
13:2;
29:5;

33:44;
39:10;
40:47, 50;
74:40, 47;
75:23.

LEARNING (KNOWLEDGE) AND SCIENCE

(a)   The urge to learning and desire for wisdom:

2:129, 151, 269;	**21:**7;
4:133;	**23:**34;
5:110;	**35:**19, 22;
6:119;	**39:**9, 10.

(b)   Learning and teaching knowledge (science):

2:159, 174;	**21:**7;
9:122;	**80:**3, 4;
16:43;	**96:**4.

(c)   Excellence of those established in learning:

3:7;	**22:**54;
4:162;	**29:**43;
10:5;	**35:**28, 32;
12:76;	**58:**11.
17:107;	

(d)   Travelling in search of knowledge:

16:75;	**68:**26;
18:60, 82;	**96:**5.

(e)   Wrong of remaining unlearned, and glorying in knowledge:

2:44;	**31:**20;
6:144;	**40:**83.
21:7;	

(f)   Science of Algebra (A.L.R, A.L.M. etc.) :

2:1;	**20:**1;
3:1;	**26:**1;
7:1;	**27:**1;
10:1;	**28:**1;
11:1;	**29:**1;
12:1;	**30:**1;
13:1;	**31:**1;
14:1;	**32:**1;
15:1;	**36:**1;
19:1;	**38:**1;

40:1;	**44**:1;
41:1;	**45**:1;
42:1;	**46**:1;
43:1;	**50**:1.

NOTE: A L R stand for Aleph, Lam and Re and A L M stand for Aleph, Lam and Mem which are the names of the Arabic letters which are found at the beginning of a number of *suras* of the Qur'an. According to Yusaf Ali in his *The Meaning of the Holy Qur'an,* published by Amana Corporation, Beltsville, Maryland, 1409AH\1989AC, they are known as the 'abbreviated letters' (p122). They are also considered as mystic symbols (p479). Ed.

(g)   Science of Astronomy and Astrology:

6:96, 97;	**35**:13;
7:45;	**36**:40;
13:2;	**37**:88;
16:16;	**41**:12;
21:23;	**53**:1, 49;
27:88;	**56**:75, 76.
31:29;	

(h)   Science of Navigation:

2:164;	**29**:65;
6:63, 97;	**30**:46;
7:64;	**31**:31;
10:22;	**35**:11, 12;
11:42;	**36**:41;
16:14;	**40**:80;
17:66, 67, 70;	**42**:32, 35;
21:82;	**43**:12;
23:22;	**45**:12.
27:63;	

(i)   Science of Geology and Mining:

16:13;	**18**:82.

Science of Surveying, Maths, etc.:

2:189;
6:96;
9:36;
10:5;
16:12;
17:12;

19:94;
30:4;
32:5;
37:5;
55:5.

Social Science:

8:46;
10:19;
16:80, 81;

18:54;
49:13;
78:8, 16.

Science of Economics:

12:47, 49, 63;
13:65;

17:29.

Science of Debate and Disputation:

2:139, 258;
3:20, 61, 66;
4:107, 109;
6:2, 25;
7:103, 171;
8:6;
18:34, 37;

21:51, 73;
22:3, 8, 9;
26:69, 89;
29:46;
31:20;
40:35;
58:1.

Industry, Art and (Industrial) Relations:

2:138;
7:148;
11:37, 38, 69;
13:17;
16:80, 92;
18:31, 96;
21:80;
22:45;

23:20;
25:10;
26:129;
27:44, 88;
29:41;
43:10, 11, 13;
55:14.

X-rays:

2:266

104:6-9.

APPENDIX

OUTLINE OF NÖLDEKE'S CHRONOLOGY OF THE QUR'AN[1]

Suras from the First Meccan Period[2]
96, 74, 111, 106, 108, 104, 107, 102, 105, 92, 90, 94, 93, 97, 86, 91, 80, 68, 87, 95, 103, 85, 73, 101, 99, 82, 81, 53, 84, 100, 79, 77, 78, 88, 89, 75, 83, 69, 51, 52, 56, 70, 55, 112, 109, 113, 114, 1

Suras from the Second Meccan Period
54, 37, 71, 76, 44, 50, 20, 26, 15, 19, 38, 36, 43, 72, 67, 23, 21, 25, 17, 27, 18

Suras from the Third Meccan Period
32, 41, 45, 16, 30, 11, 14, 12, 40, 28, 39, 29, 31, 42, 10, 34, 35, 7, 46, 6, 13

Suras from Medina
2, 98, 64, 62, 8, 47, 3, 61, 57, 4, 65, 59, 33, 63, 24, 58, 22, 48, 66, 60, 110, 49, 9, 5

---

[1] For a helpful article on the chronology of the Qur'an see Peter G. Riddell, 'Reading the Qur'an Chronologically' in *Islamic Studies Today: Essays in Honour of Andrew Rippin,* ed Majid Daneshgar & Walid A. Saleh, Brill, Leiden, 2017, pp297-316, especially p304.

[2] Ed. The list of suras (chapters) is given according to the estimated order of revelation.

www.ingramcontent.com/pod-product-compliance
Lightning Source LLC
Chambersburg PA
CBHW050743030426
42336CB00012B/1631